Palgrave Studies in Public Debt, Spending, and Revenue

Palgrave Studies in Public Debt, Spending, and Revenue is a broad-ranging and interdisciplinary series dedicated to studying the latest issues, trends, and developments influencing a government's role in its economy. The series of studies covers not only the economy's impact on government size and scope but also the effects of governmental policies on efficient allocation of resources, distribution of income, and macroeconomic stabilization. The series is also dedicated to a fuller understanding of the policies and policy tools through which government leaders develop this role, from fiscal policy to budget and various incentives that provoke particular behaviors. The subjects covered resonate in university economics, public affairs, public policy, public management, and governance schools and departments. This series' primary attention is on North America (especially the United States and Canada) and related comparative policy research. National and sub-national (including state, provincial, regional, metropolitan, and local) topics are included. At the same time, the series tracks comparable developments in China and the European Union. The series focuses on fiscal systems as influenced by the public sector and the economy, in addition to contemporary themes relating to fiscal policy, taxation, public debt, education finance, fiscal federalism, and the effects such policy designs as those found in antipoverty programs, healthcare, agriculture, and defense have on fiscal systems. Books in this series focus on research and compelling professional practices addressing public policy issues that create varying degrees of inevitability in the behavior of individuals, taxpayers, organizations, capital markets, and financial systems.

More information about this series at
https://link.springer.com/bookseries/14595

Jeffrey Chapman

The Local Budget as a Complex System

palgrave
macmillan

Jeffrey Chapman
Arizona State University
Scottsdale, AZ, USA

ISSN 2662-5148 ISSN 2662-5156 (electronic)
Palgrave Studies in Public Debt, Spending, and Revenue
ISBN 978-3-030-94902-0 ISBN 978-3-030-94903-7 (eBook)
https://doi.org/10.1007/978-3-030-94903-7

This Palgrave Macmillan imprint is published by the registered company Springer Nature Switzerland AG
The registered company address is: Gewerbestrasse 11, 6330 Cham, Switzerland

To Emmett, Jack, and Molly
There is hope for the future

Preface

This monograph is a supplement to traditional budgeting texts as well as traditional professional local budgeting guides.[1] It emphasizes that budgeting is not merely a technocratic process but rather can be examined as a complex system. While these traditional budget texts are excellent descriptions of the local budget formats, processes, and often financial management tools, they typically spend little time on the complex environment that influences the budget. While this supplement is not a budget text, by viewing the local budget through the lens of complexity, it adds a new dimension to these traditional methods of budgetary analysis. It should be noted that this monograph is designed to be brief so that the instructor of the class can easily augment this material. A complex systems framework adds to conventional budget analysis in at least four ways: It looks at the budget as the result of many variables that are outside the finance department's purview; it understands that there are multiple interdependences among these variables; it suggests analysis of non-obvious relationships among actions in the budget process in order to optimize results, and it argues that the actors in the process must understand that their budgetary behaviors have both indirect and far-reaching implications that go beyond the budget document.

[1] For texts, see Mikesell (2014), Lee et al. (2013), Lynch (2017), Menifield (2017) or Khan (2019). For a professional guide, see Opengov. (2021).

This monograph uses two concepts seldom discussed in the budgetary literature. The first is that of "governance." Following Kooiman (2003), governance is the sum of the interactions between the public and private sectors that attempt to solve societal problems and create social and economic opportunities. The second is "dynamic capabilities (or capacities)." This is the ability to change internal and external competencies in rapidly changing environments. By integrating these concepts into a complexity analysis framework, it becomes easier to understand the budget's environment, and budgeting as a practice will improve.

Note that the chapters are designed so that they can be independently read. There is some redundancy in both the subject matter and bibliographies to enable this to occur. For simplicity and understanding, the figures for each chapter are not fully complete and all of the relationships are not drawn. Finally, thanks to Molly Stoneman for help in drawing the figures.

Scottsdale, USA Jeffrey Chapman

Bibliography

Khan, A. (2019). *Fundamentals of public budgeting and finance*. Palgrave.

Kooiman, J. (2003). *Governing as governance*. Sage.

Lee, R. D., Johnson, R. V., & Joyce, P. G. (2013). *Public budgeting systems* (9th ed.). Jones & Bartlett.

Lynch, T. (2017). *Public budgeting in America* (6th ed.). Melvin & Leigh.

Menifield, C. C. (2017). *The basics of public budgeting and financial management* (3rd ed.). Hamilton Books.

Mikesell, J. L. (2014). *Fiscal administration* (10th ed.). Wadsworth.

Opengov.com/WC-2021-10-Step-Playbook-for-Quality-Budgeting-Download.html. *The 10-step playbook for quality government budgeting*. Retrieved July 8, 2021, from The_10-step_playbook_for_quality_government_budgeting.pdf.

Contents

List of Figures

CHAPTER 1

The Local Budget as a Complex System: Overview, Concepts, and Definitions

Abstract This monograph supplements traditional budgeting texts. It introduces the concepts of complexity and dynamic capacities as lenses to examine the local government budget process in a dynamic general equilibrium framework. It adds to conventional budget theory analysis by adding concepts such as fiscal sustainability, complexity analysis, a systems framework, and governance variables. It also explicitly introduces local government debt and economic development policies as budgetary variables. It uses these to analyze the potentially complex interactions of many variables on the revenue, expenditure, and debt decisions of a local jurisdiction. This framework enables the analysis of many interdependencies of exogenous variables in a complex systems framework and helps to identify some non-obvious relationships among those variables and the budget.

Keywords Fiscal sustainability · Complex systems · Governance · Dynamic capacity · Local budget

Residents of the United States have nearly constant interactions with local government. At a minimum, these interactions are, with public safety providers, health service providers, schools, zoning boards, transportation, libraries, and parks. All these services depend on the local

J. Chapman, *The Local Budget as a Complex System*,
Palgrave Studies in Public Debt, Spending, and Revenue,
https://doi.org/10.1007/978-3-030-94903-7_1

budget's revenue and expenditure characteristics. The local public budget, as adopted by the local governing board, is a concrete manifestation of the desires of the citizens of that jurisdiction. It is "where the rubber meets the road." Yet, as V.O. Key noted in 1940, "American budgetary literature is singularly arid" (Key, 1940). Forty-five years later, Straussman further argues that it is illusory to continue to search for a budgetary allocation of resources formula (Straussman, 1985). Yet, despite this theoretical vacuum, budgets do exist, and the study of budgets does continue. For example, academics study the politics of the budgetary process or study individual sections of the budget, for example, how to finance pensions, what is the incidence of the property tax, or how are debt ratings established. Practitioners focus on their own narrow turf—how can I do a better job of assessing property values, what is the forecasted sales tax revenue, how do I finance OPEBs or how to integrate risk management into management control systems (Rana et al., 2019). Further, because there are resource constraints on the revenue side and political demands on the expenditure side, budget theory has focused on micro level (that is at the individual department level or specific tax receipts) analysis of decision-making, with straightforward ratio analysis used to determine the financial position of the jurisdiction (e.g., Scorsone & Pruett, 2020).[1]

This monograph adds to the study of budgeting by analyzing the local government budget as a complex system. As such, it is only a supplement to the traditional budget texts. It will not directly address Key's and Straussman's micro level problems of resource allocation among activities. Rather it will postulate a system's theory of budgeting and derive potential implications.

Central to this discussion will be the theory of fiscal sustainability. Although Chapter 2 discusses this concept in detail, for the present it is sufficient to note that it is the long-run balanced budget, including all revenues and expenditures and influenced by a variety of other variables. Inside the fiscal sustainability box are the traditional budget phenomena of types of budgets, the various funds, and control measures. Figure 1.1 shows the variables that impact fiscal sustainability and therefore places it in a more of a general equilibrium framework. This is the contribution

[1] However, Gordon (2018) and Pagano and Hoene (2018) have attempted to broaden this micro level view.

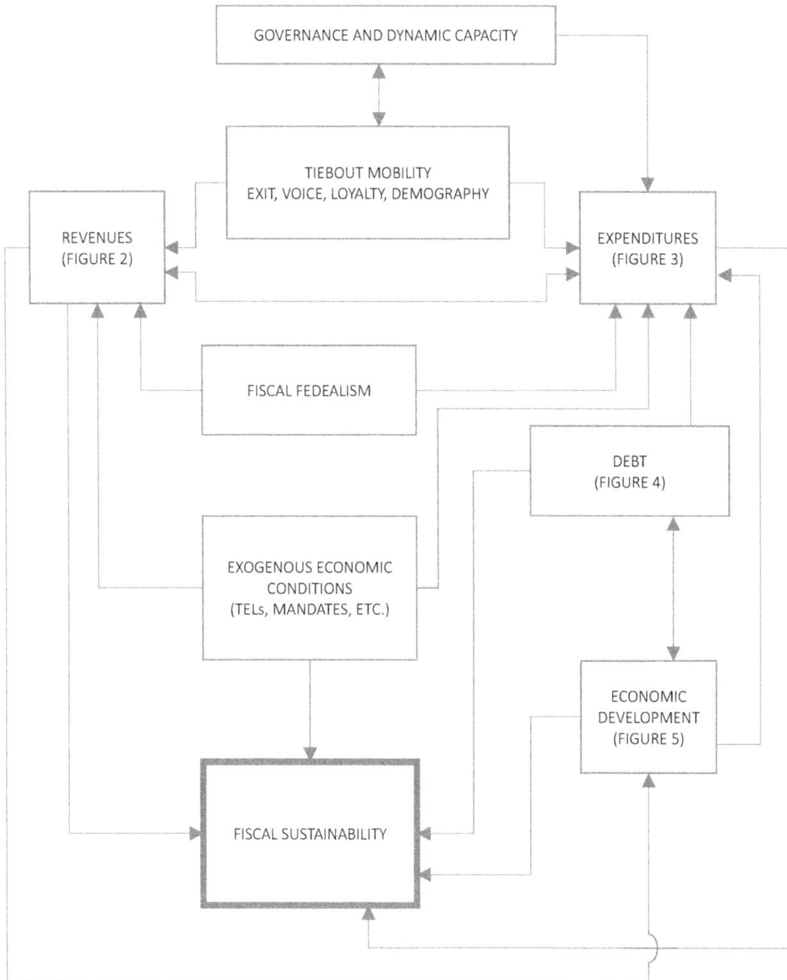

Fig. 1.1 Complex systems model

of this monograph to budgetary theory. The methodology of complex systems will be the tool to facilitate this analysis.

Just as general equilibrium theory in economics describes the economy as a whole, rather than individual markets, this monograph will describe fiscal sustainability as a product of many pressures, ranging from revenue accessibility, demand for expenditures, governance variables, managerial competence, political constraints, strategies, economic development, and so on. Fiscal sustainability does not automatically occur nor does it automatically result in local welfare maximization. But if the local decision-makers can make changes, the local budget can move to a set of resource allocations that accurately reflect these pressures and develop a budget that is fiscally sustainable and approaches welfare maximization for the local community.[2]

Additionally, the local budget is no longer a pure local budget. It is part of an intergovernmental system. As Tatham et al. (2021) argue, the territorial architecture of government has become even more multilevel, with increasing pressure on subnational governments which may face revenue constraints. Scharft (2021) elaborates on this by noting that economies of both large and small urban communities often face significant revenue shortfalls. Scharft believes that the United States has a broken fiscal federalism system, and local governments now have increased responsibilities but do not have the fiscal tools that are necessary to address these responsibilities. But perhaps using complexity analysis it will become possible to discover, understand, and address budgetary problems.

It is necessary to describe briefly complex systems before describing the budget model. These systems are the framework for the analysis of the local budget.

A system consists of coherently organized elements designed to achieve a specific purpose. These elements interconnect to achieve this purpose. A system can be more than the sum of its parts, may be resilient, and may be self-organizing (Meadows, 2008, 11–12). The study of complex systems is the study of parts of a system and how their relationships give rise to the collective behaviors of the system as well as how the system interrelates with its environment. It is a field that focuses on interdependence and the behaviors that arise from this interdependence (Bar-Yam, 2002).[3]

The study of complex adaptive systems (or complexity theory) attempts to understand how order comes about in systems that are often non-linear

[2] While many of the institutional structures used in the model may be unique to the United States, the theory is generalizable to local governments outside of the United States, assuming they have independent budget authority.

[3] For a recent example of complex systems and public policy recommendations, see Fowler et al. (2019).

and have complex relationships. At times, analysts of complexity suggest that these systems move to a state of dynamic stability, sometimes called the "edge of chaos."[4] Waldrop defines this edge of chaos as:

> *The balance point ... is where the components of a system never quite lock into place, and yet never quite dissolve into turbulence either ... the edge of chaos is where new idea and innovative genotypes are forever nibbling away at the edges of the status quo.*[5]

Complexity analysis examines a system that is constantly in motion. It often uses agency analysis to determine outcomes. It typically has four major features (Holland, 2006): many agents that interact (parallelism), agents that take actions based on the signals they receive (conditional action), groups of rules that at times combine to act as building blocks (modularity), and agents that adapt over time to improve performance (adaption). The local budget and its associated development processes have all four of these features. There are many local department heads that interact with each other as well as the private sector, the governance structure makes budget decisions based on the revenue and expenditure capabilities of the jurisdiction, budget decision-makers follow rules that are legal mandates as well as community preferences, and successful jurisdictions adapt over time to ensure they are fiscally sustainable.

Budgeting is a form of a complex system that represents a dynamic equilibrium, in which behaviors oscillate between a limited number of end states. It further contends that this system is adaptive, with many parts interacting with each other in self-organizing and dynamic ways. Additionally, it is co-evolving, in that parts of the system evolve as they interact with other parts. This is the description of the modern budget process, which is often at the edge of chaos.

There has been very little formal analysis of the local budget as a complex adaptive system. When the term "system" is sometimes used at the federal level (e.g., the planning, programing budgeting system), it is intended to be a rulebook for a systematic approach to putting together expenditure packages. While adaptive complex systems have distinct properties such as nonlinearity and feedback loops, consider this monograph as a beginning of a discussion of complexity as applied to local budgeting.

[4] In Cleveland (1994, 2).

[5] Cleveland, 2.

This differentiates it from the textbook analysis of conventional budget practice that is concerned with the technical aspects of budgeting, as well as the budget as a decision-making tool reflecting citizen interests (Franklin, 2013, 140). Traditional budgeting analysis typically examines the budget through the lens of the finance department.[6]

Thinking in a systems framework differs from conventional budget theory in at least four ways: it looks at the budget as the result of many variables that are outside the finance department's purview; it understands that there are multiple interdependences among these variables; it suggests an analysis of non-obvious relationships among actions in the budget process in order to optimize results; and it argues that the actors in the process must understand that their budgetary behaviors have indirect and far-reaching implications that go beyond the budget document. Complex adaptive systems evolve with a changing environment and should be closely linked with other systems making up the environment (Chan, 2001). Using complex system analysis contributes valuable insights that aid both budget theorists and practitioners analyze the economic and financial environment in which the budget exists.

This analysis adds two concepts to the ordinary discussion of budget models: governance and dynamic capacity (or capabilities).[7] These concepts, seldom formally emphasized in the budgeting literature, contribute to the domain of the model.

Governance

In 2016, the United Nations argued that municipal finance is the "operational fulcrum" for the success of rapid urbanization (United Nations, 2016, 2). It argues that the rules of the game are crucial to this success. It further defines the rules of the game as the statutes, policies, regulations, and laws that define a jurisdiction's powers. As part of this definition, it urges that national governments allow local governments to have autonomy over revenues and expenditures, to be in a strong intergovernmental relations framework, which includes transfers of funds from higher levels of government to localities, to have the authorization to

[6] Modern budgeting textbooks almost entirely ignore the complexity, systems design, and the simultaneity of the variables that this monograph discusses. See, for example, Mikesell (2014), Lee et al. (2013), Lynch (2017), Menifield (2017), or Khan (2019).

[7] Dynamic capability and dynamic capacity are used as synonyms in this monograph.

leverage fiscal tools, and to help localities access credit markets. It is these rules of the game that allow governance activities at the local level to exist.[8] Thus budgeting is the key to the rules of the game which defines governance.

Governance is a term that originally became popular in the mid-1990s. As originally used, it indicated that the focus on governance should be on the managerial or technocratic issues confronting local government—not on the politics of local government (Rose-Ackerman, 2017).[9] This chapter expands this definition to allow political feedback. Following Kooiman (2003), this monograph defines governance as the theoretical conception of the totality of interactions in which public and private sector actors participate in order to solve societal problems, create social and economic opportunities, and use institutions as the context for interactions.[10] For this analysis, governance includes portions of the concepts of the facilitative state, with adjustments for exogenous shocks (Newland, 2003) and the form of decision-making—for example, whether the decision-makers come from a strong mayor or strong city manager form of government, and the political climate of the jurisdiction.[11] It also includes the roles of lobbyists and private sector actors. Additionally, governance includes the political response to intergovernmental revenue flows and mandates, and the use of the Tiebout model to explain demographic changes (Tiebout, 1956).[12] Governance includes the role of the public administrator, especially in the implementation of the governing policies as well as the dynamic capabilities of the jurisdiction's management processes. This monograph's model addresses governance issues in a

[8] Interestingly, while this report discusses revenues, expenditures, and debt, it ignores economic development as an important variable.

[9] This monograph explicitly expands the idea of good governance beyond a lack of corruption.

[10] There is a vast literature expanding this definition. See, for example. Heinrich and Lynn (2000), Donahue and Nye Jr. (2001, 2002), Bertelli (2012) or Bevir (2013). Additionally, the journal *Governance* continually explores these topics.

[11] Chapter 7 expands the concept of the facilitative state in which feedback loops will be analyzed.

[12] The Tiebout model argues that under a specific set of assumptions, individuals will choose a jurisdiction that best matches their preferences for local public goods. If there are enough communities for individuals to choose from, the individual's choice of community will lead to an official market outcome. This is sometimes referred to as voting with your feet.

slightly different manner than the traditional literature (Lynn et al., 2001, 34) in that it incorporates governance issues between concepts of political interests and ahead of governance regimes, management strategies, and primary work. This model also explicitly includes feedback mechanisms. Governance issues are therefore part of a complex system rather than a stand-alone, strictly exogenous, variables. Finally, governance issues are often normative. This model assumes that while norms may be constant in the short run, they are amenable to change in the long run because of the feedback mechanisms. Under this expanded definition, it is clear that governance issues affect the budget.

Dynamic Capabilities/Capacity

The same United Nations report that commented on the importance of the rules of the game also emphasized the importance of effective financial management systems. It argues that these systems should have two dimensions: a set of core activities that include planning, budgeting, accounting, procurement auditing, and oversight; and secondly, the ability to steward their resources effectively. These are crucial attributes but are not sufficient to allow fiscal sustainability to occur. There is one more necessary attribute for fiscal stability: dynamic capability or dynamic capacity.[13]

In several sections of this monograph, the term dynamic capabilities or capacities appears as an explicit variable in the various sub-models of budgeting. This additional concept, commonly utilized in the private sector management research (Schilke et al., 2018), is rarely employed in analyzing public sector management capabilities in the finance department (Piening, 2013). Dynamic capacity is the "ability to integrate, build and reconfigure internal and external competences to address rapidly changing environments" (Teece et al., 1997), in Piening (2013, 210), Expanding on this, Eisenhardt and Martin (2000) reference the resource-based value of a firm which describes how to achieve competitive management advantage within firms and how to sustain that advantage—thus focusing on the internal organization of the firm. These authors argue that dynamic capabilities consist of specific routines that can ultimately lead to best practices. First formally advanced by Teece et al. (1997), this framework analyzes methods of fiscal success of firms in the private sector that operate

[13] These terms will be used interchangeably in this piece.

in environments of rapid technological change. It argues that private wealth accumulation creation and success in regimes of rapid technological change depend to a great degree on the sharpening of internal technological, organizational, and managerial processes within the firm, "in short, identifying new opportunities and organizing effectively and efficiently to embrace them are generally more fundamental to private wealth creation than is strategizing, if by strategizing one means engaging in business conduct that keeps competitors off balance, raises rival's costs, and excludes new entrants" (Teece et al., 519). One extension of this initial definition is to consider the assessment of the private sector firm's organizational ability to internally reconfigure to address environments that are changing in more than the use of technology to achieve innovative forms of competitive advantage. In these extensions, competition acts as one of the drivers for dynamic capability enhancement.

While becoming the prevalent theoretical framework for how private sector firms change, dynamic capability analysis has received little attention in the public management field.[14] This monograph argues that public sector organizations also face rapidly changing environments. This implies that cities will not respond uniformly to exogenous environmental shifts, but rather will respond based on their tax authority and base alignment, what tax and expenditure limits they face, and their demographic composition (Pagano & Hoene, 2018). It also argues that local governments face competition from many directions. Cities compete with other cities for economic development activities, they compete with the private sector in the production of services, they compete in the municipal bond market, and they are always justifying their activities to voters to gain approval for service or tax level changes. As Piening (2013) argues, the higher the environmental turbulence, the higher the likelihood that public organizations both invest and benefit from having dynamic capabilities (237). Importantly, he also argues that with sufficient resources, successful public organizations will develop and deploy dynamic capabilities.[15]

[14] Piening (2013) reviews 16 studies that use parts of dynamic capability analysis in the public or non-profit sector. None of these studies use complex system analysis in their discussion.

[15] For other examples of dynamic capabilities, see Teece (2007), Birkinshaw et al. (2016) and Teece et al. (2016). For contradictory evidence see Fainshmidt et al. (2019) which argues that dynamic capabilities are not important in unstable and resource poor environments but are important in resource poor but stable environments.

Figure 1.1 is a summary of the model. It hypothesizes how these variables interact with one another and how they can possibly impact the budgetary fiscal sustainability of the jurisdiction. At its center is fiscal sustainability which will be defined in more detail in Chapter 2. Underlying all the analysis is the role of the governance structure of the jurisdiction and its relationship to the jurisdiction's dynamic capabilities. The governance structure of the jurisdiction includes such factors as whether it is a strong mayor or a council-manager system since these affect the revenue and expenditure decisions of the jurisdiction (Chapman & Gorina, 2012; Jimenez, 2019). It also includes the demography of the jurisdiction, for example, jurisdictions with young families will have different demands for public services and thus result in different budgetary demands than cities with predominantly retired populations. Of course, to the extent that the Tiebout model (1956) or Hirschmanmodel (1970) are reasonably accurate, some demographic variables themselves are affected by the budgetary decisions, in that citizens will migrate to the jurisdiction that best meets their preferences for government services or will exit that jurisdiction if it changes its menu of services.[16] This mobility may affect the revenue and expenditure patterns of the jurisdiction. Tax and expenditure limits also exist at the state and local level and are part of the governance structure surrounding the local budget and both directly influence the levels of revenues and expenditures as well as having an impact on the use of special districts (Zhang, 2018).

Assuming that the "rules of the game" are met, and that governance and dynamic capacity are included explicitly as variables, six major concerns affect fiscal sustainability: revenues, expenditures, economic development, debt, the local fiscal environment, and federal and state interventions. The following chapters will discuss the first four in more detail, the next section of this chapter briefly discusses the latter two. Chapter 2 will define fiscal sustainability and why it is a useful concept as applied to budgeting. Chapter 3 analyzes the revenue system and Chapter 4 analyzes the expenditure decisions. Chapter 5 adds in a discussion of local debt and Chapter 6 analyzes local economic development activities. Chapter 7 analyzes the interdependence of these variables.

[16] The Hirschman model, originally developed to explain private sector behavior, argues that individuals have three choices if they are unhappy with the direction that the organization is taking: exit, voice, or loyalty. In the context of this monograph, it implies that over time, the jurisdiction's preferences and the individuals will be consistent.

In summary:

Revenues basically consist of local taxes, fees and charges, cash management proceeds, and intergovernmental grants. The governance system, the dynamic capabilities of that system, the local fiscal environment, and the local expenditure patterns also affect local revenues.

Expenditures are the service level costs of local programs (for example, police, parks, and libraries) and debt payments. The governance system, the local fiscal environment, and the dynamic capabilities of the governance system affect these variables. The amount of revenues raised by the jurisdiction also impacts the expenditure decisions.

Local debt occurs in a variety of forms, most of which place the local jurisdiction in a legal binding framework to pay principal and interest costs. The debt may also be related to economic development projects. Intergovernmental relationships can constrain or encourage the use of debt.

Economic Development affects both revenues and expenditures. Successful development projects will generate additional tax revenues but will also cause an increase in service expenditures. Further, to the extent that these financial incentives offered by the jurisdiction attract private sector development, there will be additional service level costs and revenue losses because of these incentives. Finally, there may be significant equity considerations attached to any development project.

The local private sector economic environment has an impact on the governance system of the jurisdiction as shown by the Tiebout and Hirschman mobility discussion. It also has a direct impact on fiscal sustainability. Poor jurisdictions will have a tax base, whether property, sales, or income, that will be less than rich jurisdictions. This means that the same tax rates will generate less revenue. This might cause poorer cities to raise taxes which could drive some of the wealthier residents of the poor jurisdiction to leave. Additionally, while the population of the poorer jurisdiction might have the same demands for public services as the population of the wealthier jurisdiction, because of the lower revenue stream, there is likely to be a lower level of service provision. It also means that poorer jurisdictions might be more willing to give incentives for economic development compared to wealthier jurisdictions.

Federal and State Interventions also affect a jurisdiction's fiscal sustainability.[17] For example, federal or state mandates may encourage or force expenditures on particular services, perhaps overriding citizen preferences. The imposition of tax limitations, for example, on property taxes, can distort local tax systems. State limitations of economic development activities can not only prevent bad decisions but also prevent what might be a good decision. However, since most of the time these interventions are beyond the control of the local government, this monograph will not address them except tangentially. This model takes the state of the national economy as a given.

Because this monograph is designed to accompany traditional budget textbooks, it does not discuss many specific budgetary phenomena that are important in the budgeting process. Any good budgeting text will discuss these topics, which are often quite technical and require detailed explanations. For example, there is no discussion of different accounting methods and financial reporting systems. It generally ignores the differentiation between capital and operating budgets. Cash management, as a revenue-generating practice, is only lightly touched. It does not analyze the politics of budget adoption nor the budget cycle. The monograph does not distinguish special funds from the General Fund, and it does not identify or analyze rainy-day funds. It does not discuss the various types of budgets—line item, performance, and program. It ignores budgetary controls and performance measures. There is no identification or analysis of the budget approval process nor are many of the actors in the budget process identified by function. These and other topics also help to shape the budget process and are traditionally covered in budgetary texts.

Bibliography

Bar-Yam, Y. (2002). *General features of complex systems (PDF). Encyclopedia of Life Support Systems*. EOLSS UNESCO Publishers. Retrieved September 16, 2014.

Bertelli, M. (2012). *The political economy of public sector governance*. Cambridge University Press.

Bevir, M. (2013). *A Theory of governance*. University of California Press.

[17] These are different from intergovernmental grants, which are direct fiscal flows, and which add to revenues or offset expenditures.

Birkinshaw, J., Zimmermann, A., & Raisch, S. (2016). How do firms adapt to discontinuous change? *California Management Review, 58*(4, Summer), 36–58.

Chan, S. (2001). *Complex Adaptive Systems*. ESD.83 Research seminar in engineering systems. Retrieved March 17, 2021, from Web.mit.edu/d.83/www/notebook/ComplexAdaptiveSystems.pdf

Chapman, J. I., & Gorina, E. (2012). Effects of the form of government and property tax limits on local finance in the context of revenue and expenditure simultaneity. *Public Budgeting and Finance, 32*(4), 19–45.

Cleveland, J. (1994, March 27). *Complexity theory: Basic concepts and application to systems thinking*. Slideshow for the Innovation Network for Communities. Retrieved August 22, 2018, from https://www.slideshare.net/johncleveland/complexity-theory-basic-concepts

Donahue, J. D., & Nye, J. S. (Eds.). (2001). *Governance amid bigger*. Brookings Institution Press.

Donahue, J. D., & Nye, J. S., Jr. (Eds). (2002). *Market-based governance*. Brookings Institution Press.

Eisenhardt, K. M., & Martin, J. A. (2000). Dynamic capabilities: What are they? *Strategic Management Journal, 21*(10–11), 1105–1121.

Fowler, P. J., Wovmand, P. S., Marcal, K. E., & Das, S. (2019, April). Solving homelessness from a complex systems perspective: Insights for prevention responses. *Annual Review of Public Health, 40*, 465–486.

Fainshmidt, S., Wenger, L., Pezeshkan A., & Mallon, M. R. (2019, June). When do dynamic capabilities lead to competitive advantage? The importance of strategic fit. *Journal of Management Studies, 56*(4), 758–787.

Franklin, A. L. (2013). Budgeting. In *Management policies in local government finance* (6th ed., 117–142). ICMA Press.

Gordon, T. (2018, September). *Predicting municipal fiscal distress: Aspiration or reality?* Lincoln Institute of Land Policy. Retrieved March 11, 2021, from https://www.lincolninst.edu/publications/working-papers/predictingmunicipal-fiscaldistress

Heinrich, C. J., & Lynn, L. E., Jr. (Eds.). (2000). *Governance and performance*. Georgetown University Press.

Hirschman, A. O. (1970). *Exit, voice, and loyalty*. Harvard University Press.

Holland, J. H. (2006). Studying complex adaptive systems. *Journal of System Science and Complexity, 19*(1), 1–8.

Jimenez, B. S. (2019). Municipal government form and budget outcomes: Political responsiveness, bureaucratic insulation and the budgetary solvency of cities. *Journal of Public Administration Research and Theory*. https//doe.org.109./jopart/musoso. Accessed 29 Aug 2019.

Key, V. O. (1940). The lack of budgetary theory. *The American Political Science Review, 34*(6), 1137–1144.

Khan, A. (2019). *Fundamentals of public budgeting and finance*. Palgrave.
Kooiman, J. (2003). *Governing as governance*. Sage.
Laurence, E. L., Jr., Heinrich, C. J., & Hill, C. J. (2001). *Improving governance*. Georgetown University Press.
Lee, R. D., Johnson, R. V., & Joyce, P. G. (2013). *Public budgeting systems* (9th ed.). Jones & Bartlett.
Lynch, T. (2017). *Public budgeting in America* (6th ed.). Melvin & Leigh.
Lynn, L. E. Jr., Heinrich, C. J., & Hill, C. J. (2001). *Improving governance: A new logic for Empirical Research*. Georgetown University Press.
Meadows, D. H. (2008). *Thinking in systems*. Chelsea Green Publishing.
Menifield, C. E. (2017). *The basics of public budgeting and financial management* (3rd ed.). Hamilton Books.
Mikesell, J. L. (2014). *Fiscal administration* (10th ed.). Wadsworth.
Newland, C. A. (2003). Newland, Chester A. 1984. *Public administration and community: Realism in the practice of ideals*. Public Administration Service.
Pagano, M., & Hoene, C. W. (2018). *City budgets in an era of increased uncertainty*. Brookings Metropolitan Policy Report.
Piening, E. P. (2013). Dynamic capabilities in public organizations. *Public Management Review, 15*(2), 209–245.
Rana T., Wickramasinghe, D., & Bracci, E. (2019). New development: Integrating risk management in management control systems—Lessons for public sector managers. *Public Money & Management, 39*(2), 148–151. Retrieved October 30, 2019, from https://doi.org/10.1080/09540962.2019.1580921
Rose-Ackerman, S. (2017, January). What does "governance" mean? *Governance: An International Journal of Policy, Administration, and Institutions, 30*(1), 23–27.
Scharft, E. (2021). Cities on their own: Local revenue when federalism fails. *Fordham Urban Law Journal, 48*(4), 919–948.
Schilke, O., Hu, S., & Helfat, C. E. (2018). Quo vadis, dynamic capabilities? *Academy of Management Annals, 12*(1), 390–439.
Scorsone, E., & Pruett, N. (2020, December 20). *Assessing existing local government fiscal early warning system through four case studies: Colorado, Louisiana, Ohio and Pennsylvania*. Michigan State University Extension, Michigan Center for Local Government Finance and Policy. Retrieved March 11, 2021.
Straussman, J. D. (1985). "The lack of a budgetary theory", where are we now? *International Journal of Public Administration, 7*(4), 345–374.
Tatham, M., Hooghe, L., & Marks, G. (2021). The territorial architecture of government. *Governance, 34*, 607–620.

Teece, D., Peteraf, M., & Leih, S. (2016). Dynamic capabilities and organizational agility: Risk, uncertainty, and strategy in the innovation economy. *California Management Review, 58*(4, Summer), 13–35.

Teece, D. J. (2007, December). Explicating dynamic capabilities: The nature and microfoundations of (sustainable) enterprise performance. *Strategic Management Journal, 28*(13), 1319–1350.

Teece, D. J., Pisano, G., & Shuen, A. (1997, August). Dynamic capabilities and strategic management. *Strategic Management Journal, 18*(7), 509–533.

Tiebout, C. M. (1956). A pure theory of local expenditures. *Journal of Political Economy, 64*(5), 416–424.

United Nations Preparatory Committee for the United Nations Conference on Housing and Sustainable Urban Development. (2016, July). Policy Paper 5: Municipal Finance and Local Fiscal Systems.

Waldrop, M. M. (1993). *Complexity: The emerging science at the edge of order and chaos*. Simon & Schuster.

Zhang, P. (2018). The unintended impact of tax and expenditure limitations on the use of special districts: The politics of circumvention. *Economics of Governance, 19*(1), 21–50.

CHAPTER 2

What Is Fiscal Sustainability?

Abstract This chapter amplifies the definition of fiscal sustainability by examining each of its parts: revenues, expenditures, debt, and employee benefits. It emphasizes that this definition is a long-run definition, with the components measured in present value terms. It discusses why the concept is important and identifies the structural pressures that affect a local government's sustainability: structural, intergovernmental, and cyclical. It then disaggregates these pressures into sub-components. These components include suburbanization, changing consumption patterns, demographic changes, and changing mobility patterns. It also notes the importance of federal and state aids on sustainability as well as business cycle pressures. It then delineates the requirements that long-run fiscal sustainability must meet, including minimizing economic distortion, attempting to raise aggregate community welfare, equity considerations,

A reminder: this monograph is not analyzing the critical budgetary details that local government finance directors routinely address. That in no way demeans their importance; rather it just means that the environment of the budget should also be explicitly addressed. For examples of the former, see Brown (1993) or GASB (2016).

J. Chapman, *The Local Budget as a Complex System*,
Palgrave Studies in Public Debt, Spending, and Revenue,
https://doi.org/10.1007/978-3-030-94903-7_2

and environmental sustainability. It finally discusses the concept's relationship with Tiebout models and equity considerations.

Keyword Fiscal sustainability · Governance · Dynamic capability · Bankruptcy

This chapter unpacks the concept of fiscal sustainability. It is a non-traditional way of examining the budget process, although it considers the same variables, that is, both revenues and expenditures (including retirement obligations). Local budgeting is usually a year-by-year process, must balance, and uses a variety of methodologies on both revenue and expenditure sides to reach its final form. Fiscal sustainability examines the same variables but in a long-run vision. So, while a local budget might use gimmicks to balance in the short run, a fiscally sustainable budget cannot use these gimmicks because it is a long-run concept.

There are some underlying concerns about the use of the term fiscal sustainability that the latter chapters in this monograph will address. To foreshadow, there are concerns about the extent of revenue and expenditure endogeneity, the existence of a powerful enough governance structure and dynamic capacity that can address mandatory and discretionary spending, and concerns about the time horizon and complex feedback mechanisms. Addressing these concerns partially connects fiscal sustainability to short-run local budgeting.

Sustainable fiscal development has three components that demonstrate complex relationships: Environmental, social, and economic (Stevens, 2005). Environmental services to society (e.g., contributions to health and living conditions) are associated with society's effects on the environment (e.g., consumption patterns). Society's effects on the economy (legal frameworks) are juxtaposed with the economy's effects on society (e.g., income levels). Further, the economy's effects on society (e.g., resource use) can offset the effects of society's variables on the economy (e.g., labor force composition). Additionally, it is possible to separate the economic component into two overlapping sectors—the public sector and the private sector. The public sector, in a federal system, consists of the national government and its subdivisions which in the United States are the state and local governments. The overlapping occurs in the realm of public–private partnerships. Together, the impacts of the interactions among these components are to change the total welfare of the inhabitants of the jurisdiction. One goal of local government, that is consistent with this welfare change is to ensure that there is an increase in fiscal sustainability. This goal underlies the entire budget process.

Fiscal sustainability is a long-run phenomena. While this chapter will later offer a more formal definition of fiscal sustainability, it can be briefly described as the government's ability to meet its expenditure commitments with its available resources over time (e.g., Burnside, 2005; Rose, 2010). This is conceptually close to the definition of environmental sustainability of economic development that development "meets the needs of the present without compromising the ability of future generations to meet their own needs." (World Commission, 1987). Seldom mentioned in the early discussions of environmental sustainability is the second part of the Commissions' definition that the sustainability requirement necessitates that the poor get a fair share of resources to sustain growth (Commission, 8). Notice that the idea of environmental sustainability pre-dates the definition of fiscal sustainability.[1]

Fiscal sustainability at the local level is important because it can energize both the public and private sectors. This occurs because with meeting the fiscal sustainability criteria, both sectors have enough resources to allow local governments to have enough fiscal autonomy to act as laboratories for implementing different public policies and for encouraging private economic growth. By focusing on both revenues and expenditures, fiscal sustainability's maintenance allows growth in dynamic capacity as well as in governance sophistication in the public sector as well as allowing the private sector to flourish.

In addition to the specific and general factors discussed in Chapter 1, there are three additional exogenous pressures that affect local government's fiscal sustainability. These pressures are structural, intergovernmental, and cyclical.

There are at least four structural pressures that can affect fiscal sustainability, on both the revenue and expenditure components. The first is suburbanization, which will affect both infrastructure demands and costs.

[1] There are a multitude of measures of severe financial stress. These are typically short-run ratios of financial variables calculated from the yearly budget. These go far beyond whether the budget is in surplus or deficit and are very valuable short-run measures (Government Accounting Stands Board, 2016). Most budgeting texts discuss these variables. However, fiscal sustainability is a long-run measure.

Suburbanization can lead to non-efficient zoning restrictions, which can lead to housing affordability problems (Ellickson, 2020). Additionally, and this is difficult to forecast, with smaller families and greater desire for urban amenities, households may prefer moving back to core cities, but, with the increasing advent of a work-from-home environment, households may desire larger homes in the suburbs. Which force will be stronger is difficult to discern. Yet, the budget implications can be large, depending upon whether the jurisdiction is growing or shrinking.

A second structural pressure would be a change in consumption patterns from the consumption of goods to the consumption of services. Since many services are untaxed, while goods are taxed, sales tax revenues will become less robust.[2] Of course, if the governance system is strong, then it is feasible to increase the sales tax base to include at least some services and thus increase sales tax revenues.

A third pressure is that of demographic change. An aging baby-boom population might lead to a shift from a full-time working (and earning higher income) population to a part-time or retired population (with lower taxable income). It may also impact local defined benefit pension plans. Conversely, if the population is younger and has more children, this could affect expenditure patterns for such government services as parks and recreation.

A fourth pressure is the constantly changing mobility patterns of both people and business. Local governments are constantly attempting to attract both. Sometimes they are successful, other times less so. In part this depends on the national economic environment, housing prices, and immigration (and immigration law) changes. These affect both the revenue and expenditure side of fiscal sustainability. There is a clear connection between these last two pressures, and they may be either offsetting or reinforcing. The finance department should be aware of these trends.

[2] Tannenwald (2004) objects to this reasoning. Tannenwald, Robert. (2003). *Are State and Local Revenue Systems Becoming Obsolete? Research Report on America's Cities*. Washington, DC: National League of Cities. Additionally, in 2018, the Supreme Court ruled in the *South Dakota v. Wayfair, Inc.* 138 S. Ct. 2080 (2018) that states may be able to charge sales taxes on purchases from out of state sellers. Many states are in the process of implementing this additional tax base.

A second exogenous set of pressures on local government is the role of the federal and state governments on local revenues and expenditures. Some of these come about through the use of mandates. Others come from secondary consequences of tax reforms; for example, the reduction of the federal estate tax affected state tax revenues which in turn, depending on state shared revenues agreements with local governments, had an impact on the local government budget (Chapman, 2008). Another example might be the national government's expansion of Medicaid which is a matching grant program which can cause distortions in local expenditures. Additionally, intergovernmental aid plays a direct role in fiscal sustainability for both cities and counties in the United States (Ji et al., 2015).[3]

A third set of pressures come from the national business cycle, primarily from the recession aspect of that cycle. For example, if there is a recession, there is a good chance that property values will be stagnant or decrease. In this case, property tax revenues will also be stagnant or decrease, even though demands for public services might increase or remain constant. If there is a recession and taxable sales fall, then that translates into a fall in sales tax revenues. While exogenous to the local budget, these macroeconomics pressures will affect its sustainability.

Even though fiscal sustainability is a long-run phenomenon, there still can be short-run budget problems. Since local governments must have a balanced budget, the budget office must confront any short-run lack of resources. The simplest, but most politically difficult way of dealing with a lack of sustainability in the short run is to raise taxes or cut expenditures. Additionally, this is also the time when budget gimmicks are instituted which are almost always counter-productive. However, in the long run, there are other opportunities for budgetary balancing solutions.

Underlying some of the potential revenue solutions is the goal of a predictable and stable set of revenue sources, implying a system of diverse revenues that in the aggregate are less volatile. The governance system must show some dynamic capacity in making these revenue choices. Governments can examine existing revenue sources, perhaps expanding the tax base and eliminating some exemptions or deductions. This is

[3] However, not all intergovernmental activities have an effect on sustainability. Yang (2019) finds that if one major jurisdiction declares bankruptcy, it has no effect on the borrowing costs of nearby jurisdictions.

especially true for property taxes. Another revenue action might be developing or enhancing revenue sources—for example, using privatization techniques or increasing the use of fees and charges. Governments can also tinker with expenditures—perhaps changing a pure pension benefit system to a hybrid benefit-define contribution system. Another solution would be to mandate the financing of a "rainy-day" fund that can offset cyclical declines in revenues as well as cyclical increases in expenditures.

There are also some short-run actions which are truly ad hoc and are not sustainable in the long run. For example, the "roll over" in which the government pays bills one day into the next fiscal year, allowing the current fiscal year to balance. Another is to issue short-term debt. A third is to beg the higher level of government (typically the state, but sometimes the national government) to give more aid. This last set of short-run solutions will not lead to long-run fiscal sustainability and the jurisdiction should avoid using them unless the fiscal situation is crucial. Since the ultimate solution to fiscal sustainability problems is to ensure that the electorate understands that there is no such thing as a "free lunch," these tactics can easily mislead the public (and perhaps the city council) into believing that there are no long-run fiscal problems.

Given these caveats, a more formal definition of long-run fiscal sustainability is the following:

The sum of the present value of the interest on the jurisdiction's debt payments (both principal and interest) plus the present value of the jurisdiction's expenditures plus the present value of the jurisdiction's pension payments plus the present value of the jurisdiction's other post-employment benefits (OPEBs) minus the present value of the jurisdiction's total revenues must be less than or equal to zero.[4]

This is a present value, that is a long-run, equation. If the solution is greater than zero, it means that in the long run, total expenditures (including pensions and OPEBs) exceed total revenues. This implies that there is a lack of fiscal sustainability, and the jurisdiction must make changes in its budgetary patterns in order to avoid bankruptcy. It is this definition that is the center of this monograph. It assumes that jurisdictions are not inherently stable in the short run but rather are

[4] See Chapman (2015) for a more formal definition. If the result is less than zero, the jurisdiction is running a surplus.

subject to various changes in inputs and outputs.[5] However, in the long run, there must be a stable solution, or the local government will go bankrupt.[6] While local bankruptcy may not always be harmful to the overall fiscal health of the state, it does come with trade-offs including breaking promises to public sector workers, bond holders, and other creditors (Abott & Singla, 2021).

Further, there is no reason why this fiscal sustainability must be at an optimal community welfare location, assuming that a social welfare function exists.[7] The following chapters will closely examine the determinants of revenues, expenditures, and debt for potential changes. The national economy determines the discount rate for the present value calculations, and the governance system and the level of public sector employment set the amount of pension and OPEBs expenditures.[8]

One implicit assumption in this analysis is that it is possible to estimate the future levels of revenues, expenditures, debt, and employee benefits. For debt, this is difficult, but not insolvable. Debt schedules are known. It is only new debt (or new debt instruments) that introduces uncertainty. The same reasoning can be employed in estimating future public benefits financed by the debt. However, revenues and expenditures are more problematic.

Kavanagh (2007), in a detailed analysis, explains that forecasting expenditures should examine four cost elements: personnel services, commodities (which are non-capital goods), debt service, and interfund

[5] This sustainability definition contains both normative and positive analysis. Normative in the sense that it assumes that local governments have the political power to make revenue and expenditure decision and they should use that power to reach and maintain fiscal sustainability. Positive in the sense that under the current legal system, this definition must hold over time—it is definitional not political.

[6] Empirically, municipal bankruptcy seldom occurs. Excluding dismissed bankruptcy filings, only eight localities out of 2710 successfully filed for bankruptcy between 2008 and 2018 (Maciag, 2013). For comparison purposes, there were 389,278 commercial bankruptcy filings during this same period. Further, as Yang (2019) has shown, there is no support for the hypothesis that a general contagion to other local governments arising from a municipal bankruptcy.

[7] This analysis will also occur later in this monograph.

[8] Fiscal sustainability is related but different from the Pagano and Hoene (2018) description of the fiscal policy space of cities. Their paper is more concerned about the constraints that face jurisdictions when they attempt to carry out new, exogenous, mandates, or raise revenues. These clearly affect fiscal sustainability but do not define it.

transfers. He then identifies methods for forecasting new operating expenditures, including the operating costs of new capital assets and then the costs of operating new services or programs. He then describes the importance of forecasting non-current liabilities including maintenance, pensions (including OPEBS), and accrued employee time-off. Kavanaugh also describes long-term revenue forecasting techniques, including judgmental, historical trend analysis regression analysis, and hybrid techniques. He notes that using more sophisticated statistical techniques does not necessarily lead to better estimates and the simplest technique that generates accurate and understood projections is recommended, Kavanagh recommends that the jurisdiction should develop an explicit revenue model, disaggregate revenue projections, if possible, data should be known, that collaboration with other experts outside of the jurisdiction should be considered, and technology should be effectively used. Additionally, Thompson and Gates (2007) claim that accurately predicting revenue growth is close to impossible because revenues are primarily driven by economic growth.[9] There has been some recent discussion on revenue forecasting (e.g., Mikesell, 2018; Rueben & Randall, 2017) with Mikesell concluding that in the long run, the forecasts are reasonable. However, estimating steams of expenditures has not really proved successful, and often cities use simple time series trends.[10]

There are two other important concerns. First, if jurisdictions are overly cautious or overly optimistic, the forecasted revenues and expenditures will be biased. In these cases, the jurisdiction may be undertaking unnecessary cutbacks in services or raising taxes unnecessarily. Second, it is likely that small jurisdictions do not necessarily have the internal capabilities of undertaking sophisticated financial projections. Here is where the dynamic capacity of the jurisdiction may play an important role.[11]

Long-run fiscal sustainability should also meet the following requirements:

[9] Thompson and Gates's analysis is far more sophisticated, involving the modern financial theory concepts of variance and drift.

[10] The interest rate is not necessarily the same discount rate used by pension boards to determine the present value of the pension liability. It is sometimes politically determined (Wang & Peng, 2018).

[11] The interest rate is not necessarily the same discount rate used by pension boards to determine the present value of the pension liability. It is sometimes politically determined (Wang & Peng, 2018).

- The tax instruments used to raise revenues should minimize economic distortion. That is, they should not significantly change taxpayer's behavior.
- The sustainability solution must attempt to raise aggregate community welfare.
- There must be consideration of the equity impacts of changing expenditure patterns and revenue raising activities.
- Environmental sustainability is an important constraining factor.

This monograph focuses on the complexity of the budget-making process so these constraints will not be specifically addressed. This does not mean these are unimportant, but rather they are a step removed from the purview of the finance department.

While not formally included in the definition, dynamic capacity and governance concerns are important in the analysis. As Fig. 1.1 shows, these two concepts are interrelated. When applied to fiscal sustainability, it may be that if, in the short run, the jurisdiction is in fiscal trouble, it may become entrepreneurial because of necessity. Or a jurisdiction may need to have excess resources to give it the ability to take risks. While much of the literature examining these conflicting actions is more than twenty years old, Singla et al. (2018) find that resource constraints are associated with entrepreneurial activity in the United States. Interestingly, their results might indicate that dynamic capacity may be unrelated to the governance system (as indicated by strong mayor or strong manager dichotomy). Brookings (Escobari & Seyal, 2020) implicitly urges that cities use their dynamic capacity to bolster economic development and work in partnerships with firms and community stakeholders to successfully build the capabilities that the firms require—a result consistent with facilitative state analysis. Chapter 6 will examine economic development as a separate component of fiscal sustainability.

In addition to the fiscal survival of the jurisdiction, there may be at least three other reasons why fiscal sustainability is important. The first is its relationship with the Tiebout model. This model postulates a large number of cities within a metropolitan area that has different levels and types of taxation and public service provision. If these jurisdictions are not fiscally sustainable, then it will be difficult, if not impossible, to reach a long-run Tiebout local optimum. A second reason is that non-fiscally sustainable jurisdictions may be more willing to ignore equity considerations as they attempt to reach sustainability. Service cuts may affect the poor or regressive taxes implemented. For example, Brien et al. (2021) find that human services bear the most significant share of expenditure reductions under continuing fiscal stress. Note though that once a city becomes long-run fiscally sustainable, it may be able to take actions that mitigate these discriminatory activities.

The third reason is that cities will engage in many activities in order to be fiscally sustainable. For example, the Government Finance Officers Association (Carlson & Olivares, 2021; Kavanagh, 2020) devotes large portions of their journal to bringing revenues and expenditures into alignment and determining priorities in budgeting decisions. While implicitly recognizing the complex nature of budgeting, in neither case do they explicitly incorporate complexity issues. However, Warner et al. (2021), using slightly different terminology, demonstrate that many jurisdictions have some dynamic capabilities as they respond differentially to fiscal stress. Some engage pragmatically by employing differential responses such as cuts, deferrals, and adding revenues. These responses reflect governance activities as well. However, they ignore complexity type analysis.

While the next four chapters disaggregate the model into revenues, expenditures, debt, and economic development, all are only interconnected parts of the fiscal sustainability equation. There will be many interlocked moving elements in the discussion, but all are central to fiscal sustainability.

Bibliography

Abott, C., & Singla, A. (2021, May/June). Helping or hurting? The efficacy of municipal bankruptcy. *Public Administration Review, 81*(3), 428–445.

Brien, S., Eger III, R. J., & Matkin, D. S. T. (2021, May/June). The timing of managerial responses to fiscal stress. *Public Administration Review, 81*(3), 414–427.

Brown, K. W. (1993). The 10-point test of financial condition: Toward an easy-to-use assessment tool for smaller cities. *Government Finance Review, 9*(6), 21–26.

Burnside, C. (Ed.). (2005). *Fiscal sustainability in theory and practice*. The World Bank.

Carlson, J., & Olivares, K. (2021, April). Prioritizing your values. *Government Finance Review, 37*(2), 18–37.

Chapman, J. I. (2008). The fiscalization of land use: The increasing use of innovative revenue raising instruments to finance public infrastructure. *Public Works Management and Policy, 12*(4), 551–567.

Chapman, J. I. (2015). Fiscal sustainability. In M. Dubnick & D. Bearfield (Eds.), *Encyclopedia of public administration and public policy* (3rd ed., pp. 1486–1494). Taylor & Francis Group.

Ellickson, R. C. (2020, January 13). *Zoning and the cost of housing: Evidence from Silicon Valley, greater New Haven, and greater Austin.* Available at SSRN. Retrieved June 2, 2021, from https://ssrn.com/abstract=3472145 or http://dx.doi.org/10.2139/ssrn.3472145

Escobari, M., & Seyal, I. (2020). *3 ways cities can redefine their economic trajectories.* Brookings blog. Retrieved February 27, 2020, from www.brookings.edu/blog/up-front/2020/02/25/3-ways-cities-can-redefine-their-economic-trajectories

Government Accounting Standards Board. (2016, July 21). *Indicators of severe financial stress and going concern disclosures.* Retrieved July 6, 2021.

Ji, H., Ahn, J., & Chapman, J. (2015, August). The role of intergovernmental aid in defining fiscal sustainability at the sub-national level. *Urban Studies.* http://usj.sagepub.com/content/early/2015/08/26/0042098015600?papetoc

Kavanagh, S. (2020, August). Balancing the budget in bad times. *Government Finance Review, 30*(4), 34–65.

Kavanagh, S. C. (2007). *Financing the future: Long-term financial planning for local government.* Government Finance Officers Association.

Maciag, M. (2013). How rare are municipal bankruptcies? *Governing.* Retrieved December 6, 2018, from https://www.governing.com/archive/municipal-bankruptcy-rate-and-state-law-limitations.html

Mikesell, J. L. (2018, September/October). Often wrong, never uncertain: 40 years of state revenue forecasting. *Public Administration Review, 78*(5), 795–802.

Pagano, M., & Hoene, C. W. (2018). *City budgets in an era of increased uncertainty.* Brookings Metropolitan Policy Report.

Rose, S. (2010, December). Institutions and fiscal sustainability. *National Tax Journal, 63*(4), 807–838.

Rueben, K. S., & Randall, M. (2017, November 28). *Revenue forecasting practices: How states estimate future revenues.* Tax Policy Center. Retrieved April 3, 2021, from http://www.taxpolicycenter.org/publications/revenue-forecasting-practices/full

Singla, A., Stritch, J., & Feeney, M. K. (2018). Constrained or creative? Changes in financial condition and entrepreneurial orientation in public organizations. *Public Administration, 96*, 1–18.

Stevens, C. (2005, September). *Measuring sustainable development* (Organization for Economic Co-operation and Development No. 10).

Tannenwald, R. (2004). Are state and local revenue systems becoming obsolete? *Research Report on American Cities*. National League of Cities.

Thompson, F., & Gates, B. (2007, September–October). Betting on the future with a cloudy crystal ball? How financial theory can improve revenue forecasting and budgets in the states. *Public Administration Review, 67*(5), 825–836.

Wang, Q., & Peng, J. (2018, September/October). Political embeddedness of public pension governance: An event history analysis of discount rate changes. *Public Administration Review, 78*, 785–794.

Warner, M. E., Aldag, A. M., & Kim, Y. (2021, May/June). Pragmatic municipalism: U.S. local government responses to fiscal stress. *Public Administration Review, 81*(3), 389–399.

World Commission on Environment and Development. (1987). *Our common future*. Oxford University Press.

Yang, Y. (2019, September). Negative externality of fiscal problems: Dissecting the contagion effect of municipal bankruptcy. *Public Administration Review, 79*(2), 156–167.

CHAPTER 3

The Revenue Module

Abstract Local government revenue sufficiency has been a long studied problem. This chapter analyzes the revenue sources for the jurisdiction. It identifies a variety of sources—property taxes, sales taxes, grants, fees and charges, cash management returns, employee contributions and other sources. It discusses equity issues, incentives for revenues, and constraints on revenues. It discusses tax base issues, tax innovations such as tax increment financing and community facilities districts, and the importance of land use decisions. It examines the impact of revenues on expenditures and vice versa. The chapter demonstrates both the complexity of the revenue system and how dynamic capabilities have generated new revenue sources that have added to this complexity.

Keyword Taxes · Fees and charges · Incidence · Intergovernmental transfers

Revenue scarcity has long been an on-going discussion in urban public finance; for example, forty years ago there was an entire issue of *Public Administration Review* dedicated to this topic (McCaffery (ed.), 1981). Figure 3.2 is an expansion of the revenue module of Fig. 3.1 and is still a simplification of an even more complex system.

J. Chapman, *The Local Budget as a Complex System*,
Palgrave Studies in Public Debt, Spending, and Revenue,
https://doi.org/10.1007/978-3-030-94903-7_3

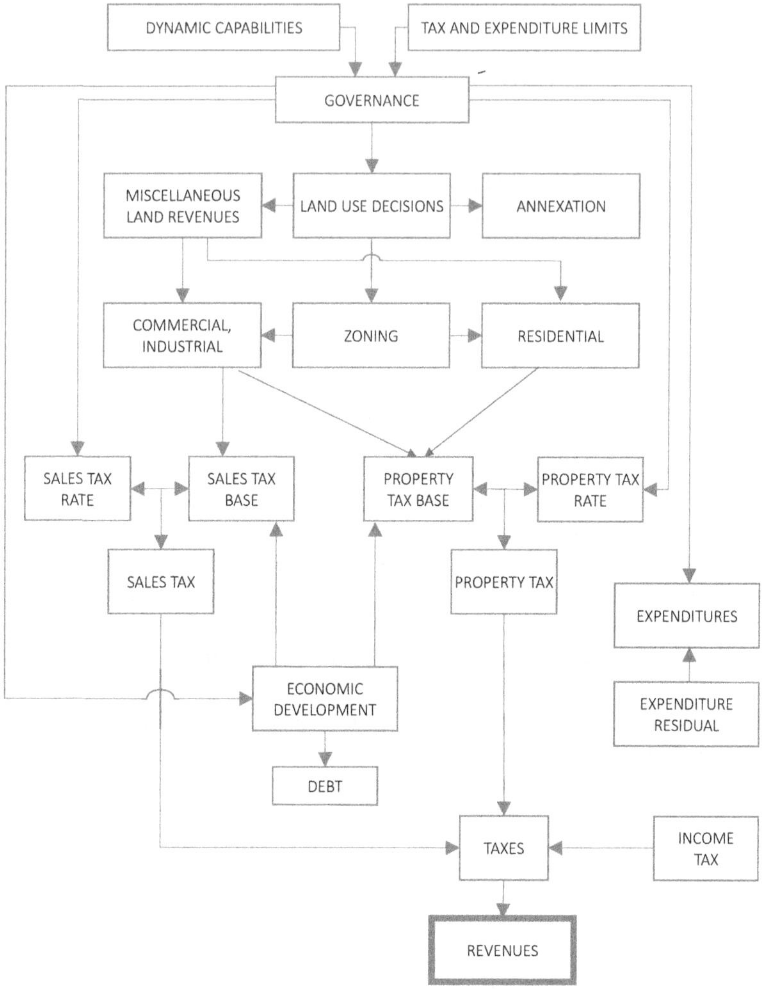

Fig. 3.1 Revenues

As Fig. 3.2 shows there are five primary sources of revenues that are direct inputs into the total revenues of the jurisdiction: taxes, intergovernmental transfers from the state and federal government, employee contributions for pensions and Other Post-Employment Benefits (OPEBs),

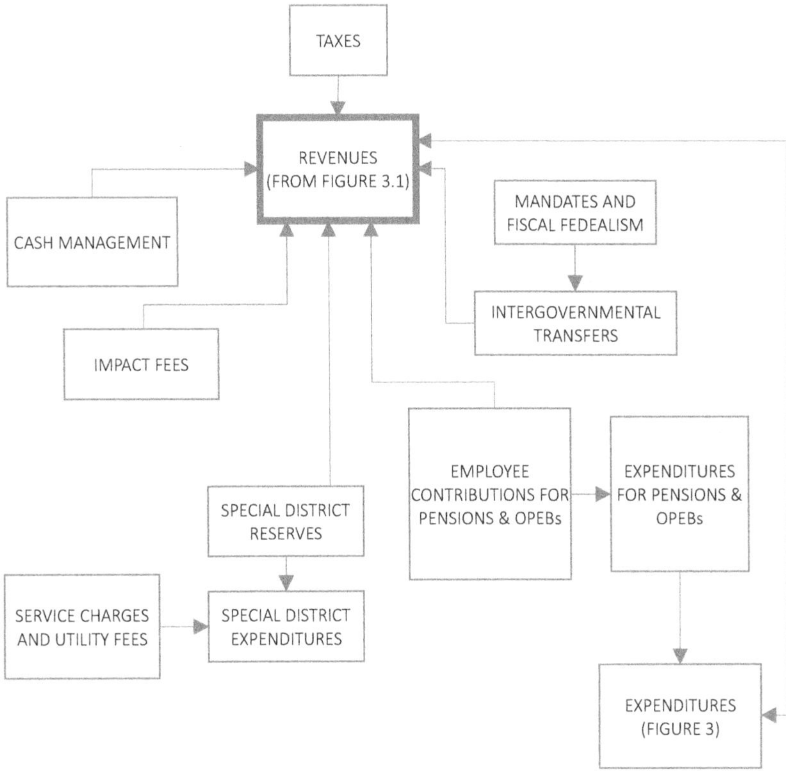

Fig. 3.2 Revenues (continued)

special district revenues (which can include service charges and utility fees, and revenues from cash management).[1] Additionally, there are differences in revenue systems among cities, which can influence the fiscal health of the jurisdiction (Chernick, 2017).

Figure 3.1 illustrates the complexity of the tax system. It hypothesizes that the governance system, as partially determined and limited by the dynamic capacity of the jurisdiction as well as the tax and expenditure limits that constrain the jurisdiction lead to a variety of decisions

[1] There are many other small sources of revenues that will not be considered in this analysis.

that ultimately affect tax revenues. Figure 3.1 notes the importance of land use decisions; however, there are a myriad of other decisions not illustrated in the diagram (for example, neighborhood pressures, macroeconomic effects, and the political beliefs of the political decision makers).[2] Figure 3.2 depicts the complexity of other sources of revenue in addition to taxes. For the most part, these sources are of secondary importance to the total jurisdictional revenues. The rest of this chapter will discuss some selected influences on revenues.

The top part of Fig. 3.1 illustrates the complexity of the tax system. It hypothesizes that the governance system, as partially determined and limited by the dynamic capacity of the jurisdiction as well as the tax and expenditure limits that constrain the jurisdiction, leads to a variety of decisions that ultimately affect tax revenues. This portion of Fig. 3.1 emphasizes the importance of land use decisions; however, there are a myriad of other decisions not illustrated in the diagram (for example, neighborhood pressures, macroeconomic effects, and the political beliefs of the political decision-makers). The bottom part of Fig. 3.1 depicts the complexity of other sources of revenues. For the most part, these sources are of secondary importance to the total jurisdictional revenues. The rest of this chapter will discuss some selected influences on revenues.

There are a variety of governance issues that influence the collection of revenues. As earlier noted, strong mayor governments have different effects on revenue/expenditure patterns than city manager led governments. Local governments also affect revenues through their land use powers (Chapman, 1988). For example, by zoning for commercial or industrial use rather than residential use, they determine differential property values and therefore property tax revenues, the amount of potential sales and therefore sales tax revenues, and different residential densities and therefore different household property tax liabilities. It is not unusual for cities to consider the fiscal impacts of various land uses and then make land use decisions based on those impacts (Chapman, 2008).

Additionally, land use decisions can have an effect on the demographic characteristics of the jurisdiction which will affect the jurisdiction's revenues. For example, large lot zoning will lead to more expensive

[2] Note that not all the connections are illustrated in order to keep Fig. 3.2 intelligible.

housing which will lead to more higher income residents.[3] Felix (2008) has estimated the long-run sales tax elasticity to be 0.92, so that a ten percent increase in income would lead to a 9.2 percent increase in sales tax revenues.

Depending upon the dynamic capacity of local decision-makers, local government can encourage (or discourage) economic development activity, typically using incentives, which can also affect local revenues as well as expenditures. As Fig. 3.1 illustrates another exogenous governance issue is the existence of tax and expenditure limits (TELs). While typically instituted at the state level, often by voter initiatives, there are examples of city TELs (Brooks et al., 2016). These typically act to constrain the amount of taxes that local governments can increase. Additionally, it may be that political-based annexation decisions have effects on the spreading of the tax base (Wang & Gorina, 2018). The extent of these governance activities reflects the dynamic capability of the jurisdiction—successful innovations in this arena will lead to a greater likelihood of fiscal sustainability.

There are three basic blocks of taxes: sales taxes, property taxes, and other taxes, which are primarily local income taxes. Since only eleven states have local income taxes, and they raise very little revenue for localities when implemented, this chapter will not analyze them.[4] This chapter will later examine fees and charges which, while not taxes, generate a large part of local revenues.

Equity concerns are also important when discussing taxes. A tax is regressive if it takes a greater percentage of income from the poor than the wealthy; it is proportional if it takes the same percentage of income from the poor and the wealthy, and it is progressive if it takes a higher percentage of income from the wealthy than the poor. Note that these are percentages, not absolute levels. It is sometimes difficult to calculate the incidence of a tax—that is who is the ultimate payer of the tax; however, the finance department should warn the decision-makers if the tax is regressive so that they can anticipate political feedback.

[3] Large lot or even single-family zoning is a contribution to the affordable housing crises which many cities are experiencing.

[4] However, just because they do not raise much money does not mean that they should be ignored. It may be that this is an unexplored arena for local revenue.

Sales Taxes

There are two types of sales taxes. The base of an *excise* type sales tax is the volume of sales, e.g., a tax per gallon of gasoline. The base of an *ad valorem* sales tax is the value of the sale, and the tax is a percentage, e.g., a five percent tax on beer. Most sales tax revenues come from the *ad valorem* type. Thirty-six states allow the implementation of local sales taxes. Its importance varies among the states—some localities receive as much as 30 percent of their total local tax revenue, while others receive virtually nothing (Mikesell, 2018).

While it should be straightforward to determine the base of the sales tax, there are some relationships and decisions that make it more complex. First, it is dependent on the composition of the establishments that generate the sales—for example, a diamond store might generate more sales taxes than a larger furniture store. Second, the amount of land available for commercial use is dependent upon the zoning that the jurisdiction makes available for commerce. Third, the determination of the base is sometimes a political decision—for example, should there be a sales tax on services and if so, which services. Or should there be a sales tax on food? Fourth, sales tax experts generally agree that local sales taxes be state administered and should have a base that is identical to the state sales tax (Mikesell, 2013). Finally, how to tax internet sales is sometimes a question. Also note that economic development decisions are sometimes based on the anticipated sales tax revenues that the development will generate, so that there are both governance issues and dynamic capacities issues involved in determining increments to the base.

Typically, local sales tax rates are in addition to the state's sales tax rate, which is constant across the jurisdictions in the state. There may be some variability among local rates if the state allows them to be set by the local government. Local governments set these rates based on the rates of adjacent cities and the necessity for additional revenue to fund local services. This is an example of how local expenditures can indirectly affect total local revenues (see Fig. 1.1).

Often people believe that the incidence of the sales tax is on the consumer, and since low-income consumers spend a greater percentage of their income on consumption goods, they will pay a higher percentage of their income in taxes. This makes the sales tax a regressive tax. However, there are some caveats to this analysis. In particular, the elasticities of supply and demand for the taxed product are important in determining the amount of the tax that the consumer pays and what the consumer buys is also important. For example, suppliers of goods that face a highly inelastic demand are likely to be able to shift more of the tax to the consumer; or taxes on goods that low-income consumers are unlikely to purchase (e.g., yachts) are unlikely to be regressive.

Property Taxes

There are many advantages to the property tax. Unlike an income tax which requires a deep understanding of the very complex tax laws or a sales tax under which it is difficult to determine the total amount of taxes paid in a year because of the multiplicity of transactions that generate sales tax payments, the property tax is a lump sum payment, clearly visible to the taxpayer, either through its appearance on mortgage payment statements or through the receipt of a property tax bill. It is also a relatively stable source of tax revenues for local governments—land is not mobile, and structures are mobile only in the long run. Finally, the portion of the tax on land is efficient because the supply of land will not change when the jurisdiction implements the tax. For a variety of political and economic reasons, today's property tax is primarily a tax on structures and land. Roughly, the property tax provides about a quarter of local revenues and over 70 percent of local taxes (Chapman, 2013).

The first step in property tax administration is the appraisal of the property. This is the determination of the value of the property. Methods to do this include comparable property sales, individual on-site evaluation, or computer-assisted mass appraisal (using regression analysis). Unfortunately, unless the property has recently sold, these appraisals can be inaccurate, which has sometimes resulted in gross inequities. In some jurisdictions, the assessor deliberately lowers the calculated value of the property so there will be few complaints about over assessment. Once the property value is determined, it is subject to the calculation of its taxable value, which essentially is the property tax base. This calculation can become extremely complex. For example, there are nine different classes of property in Arizona, with nine different assessment ratios.[5] Because of

[5] Mines, agriculture, residential, residential rental, railroad and airline flight property, non-commercial historic property (including foreign trade zone property and enterprise zone property), historic commercial and industrial property, residential rental historic

this, the same tax rate will generate different amounts of tax revenue for similarly appraised value.

The tax rate is set by the governing body, typically in the context of a public hearing. In most states, tax limitation laws limit this rate setting. Underlying much of the public discussion is the need for a certain level of revenues to sustain a desired level of public expenditures. Many jurisdictions publish the calculated rate before formally adopting it. Finally, the rate multiplied by the base (after adjusted for its property class) generates the property tax revenues for the city.

The property tax is more complex to analyze than other taxes. Median voter models assert that the level of expenditures in the jurisdiction is a function of the property tax rate (Bergstrom & Goodman, 1973). Thus, indirectly, the median voter determines the level of property taxes. Conversely, as Brien (2018) and Ross (2018) have shown, there exists a property tax residual—that is for some services, an expenditure is first determined, then the jurisdiction utilizes other revenue sources to help fund the service and finally, the jurisdiction calculates the property tax bill to fill in any gap. In these cases, expenditure levels help to determine the property tax revenue levels that the local government needs.

One particular variable that impacts property tax revenues through its effects on the base is zoning—an instrument of land use decision-making that the planning department of the jurisdiction oversees, and which the governance system of the city ultimately adopts. For example, as the city moves to more zoning for commercial properties, this changes the property value and thus property tax receipts for those parcels. Fiscally stressed jurisdictions may change these zoning regulations to encourage economic development, or they may be based on fiscal issues rather than economic welfare issues (Chapman, 2008). In some jurisdictions, large lot zoning has constricted the supply of housing, leading to higher than expected prices in the housing market (Ellickson, 2020). Additionally, since economic development projects are often debt financed, these have an influence on the total property tax rate, causing an increase in the rate necessary to finance the debt. Land use decisions and city budgets are therefore interrelated (Chapman, 1988). Finally, as the property base increases, it becomes possible to decrease the tax rate while

property and possessory interest, and real property (Arizona Tax Research Association, 2016).

maintaining the same level of public expenditures. Since most jurisdictions face an increasing demand for expenditures, this usually means that the tax rate does not have to increase as much to finance the higher level of expenditures.

Determining the incidence of the property tax can be complex. The simplest part to determine is the tax on land. This is clearly progressive—wealthy people own more land than poor people, and there is no behavior that can shift the tax because land is in fixed supply. The incidence of the tax on structures is the cause for some debate. The traditional view is that the owner of the residence pays the property tax (or paid by the renter in the case of rentals), and it is regressive, since poor people spend a greater proportion of the income on housing than rich people. The tax on business structures depends on the opportunity to shift the tax forward to consumers (regressive) or backwards to suppliers and labor (also regressive). Therefore, the tax is regressive. A second view (called the "new" view) comes to a different conclusion. This new view claims that since nearly all cities have a property tax, it can it is best thought of as a national tax on capital. Since rich people own more capital than poor people, the property tax is likely to be progressive. This "new" view has become the commonly accepted view among most public finance economists. A final view is that there exists an entirely different interpretation of the tax. In this case, the tax is a payment for a specific bundle of goods and services financed by the tax. This is the benefit view and is consistent with the Tiebout hypothesis. In this case, incidence studies make little sense—somewhat similar to asking "what is the incidence of the price of an apple." Generally, most economists believe that while the property tax, as implemented, is an imperfect tax, it has both a progressive element and a benefit element.[6]

There can be a close relationship between the property tax and economic development. There are at least four specific examples of this relationship.

A tax on land, at least in theory, might stimulate more intense development. This occurs for two reasons. The first is that a land tax does not change the amount of land in the jurisdiction. Its incidence is strictly on the owner of the land. To pay this tax, the owner needs to develop some income-producing asset, typically some structure, built on that land. The

[6] See Youngman (2016) for a more detailed and straightforward analysis of the incidence discussion.

higher the tax, the more development should occur. There has been some empirical work (Oates & Schwab, 1997) that seems to indicate that this theoretical proposition may have some validity. *Value Capture taxes* are closely related to land taxes and are a useful measure of financing infrastructure improvements. In these cases, the jurisdiction calculates the value of the property prior to the announcement of an infrastructure improvement that could increase this value. As developers build improvements, and the land value increases, a portion of this increase in value is captured by a tax designed to finance the infrastructure that is responsible for this increase in value. Many developing countries have used this technique to finance local infrastructure improvements (Smolka, 2012).

Closely related to a value capture tax is a technique known as *tax increment financing (TIF)*. This is a technique that is extraordinarily popular in the United States, with only Arizona and California not authorizing its use.[7] This technique involves drawing a line around a specific geographic area and then determining the taxes that the area is currently generating. This is the initial tax base. Then, the jurisdiction improves the area typically through infrastructure improvements. It finances this improvement by issuing debt. Debt and interest payments come from taxing the increment in property value that occurs because of the improvements. Originally developed to improve blighted areas, the use of TIFs quickly expanded to redevelop non-blighted areas. Finally, other districts dependent on increases in property values, especially school districts, believe that they were not getting their fair share of the increment and often protest.

A final example is that of a *Community Facility District*.[8] These are special taxing districts, typically advanced by a developer and authorized by the local government. They serve as a mechanism to finance improvements, in both capital infrastructure and services within a specified area. In these Community Facilities Districts, the property tax is an excise tax rather than an ad valorem tax, typically based on the characteristics of the property. Often, these are residential areas that the jurisdiction could not afford to provide the necessary infrastructure such as streets and sewers or services such as garbage collection by themselves.

[7] In California, Enhanced Infrastructure Financing Districts have replaced TIFs (Horiuchi & Chapman, 2019).

[8] Called Mello-Roos Districts in California.

For Tax Increment Financing Districts and Community Facilities Districts, there is no general vote by the public so these are sometimes controversial.

Local Income Taxes

The income tax is usually unimportant at the local level, bringing in about 2 percent of total local revenues (Chapman, 2013). There is usually little coordination or conformity between local income taxes and state income taxes. Local finance departments administer these local income taxes. The base of this tax is typically only wages and salaries, thereby ignoring other sources of income. The incidence is on the employee and a major concern is where the income is earned or where the individual lives (Mikesell, 2013).

Intergovernmental Transfers

As noted in the introduction to this chapter, there are several non-tax sources of revenue for local governments. The first is intergovernmental grants and transfers—that amount of money that comes from the state or federal government. This is a substantial part of the revenues that local governments receive—about 30 percent (Chapman, 2013) most of this money comes from the state, although in some cases, the state is merely acting as a transfer agent from the federal government.

One theoretical justification for these transfers and grants is based on Oates' decentralization work (Oates, 1972). Essentially, Oates argues that the decisions concerning the provision of public services should be determined by the demands for these services by the residents of the respective jurisdiction. That is, the national government should provide such services as defense and local governments should provide such services as police. Grants ensure that there is enough financial ability at the subnational or sub-state level to provide these services.

Grants can be of several types. Conditional grants mandate that the grant funds must be used for a particular service; an unconditional grant has no mandate. For example, a grant from the state to the local police department for patrol cars must be spent on patrol cars is an example of a conditional grant. State revenue sharing with the local government is typically unconditional. A matching grant has the provision that the local government provides a certain percentage of the revenue in order to receive the grant. Finally, a grant may be open-ended or closed-ended. An open-ended grant means that if the criteria for the grant continue to exist, the grant money flows. A closed-ended grant means that after spending a specified sum, there is no more money. An example of an open-ended grant might be education expenditures based on the number of students—as long as the students show up, the money flows. In most cases, an open-ended matching grant is the appropriate form (Oates, 1972). There are two important grant caveats. First, money is fungible, so a grant for one purpose might free up funds that now are available for a different purpose. In the above example of patrol cars, the local funds budgeted for those cars can now finance other police necessities. Second, grants are very difficult to track (Randall et al., 2018). A particular department might be receiving grant money from several different sources which then are intermixed, or accounting methods may differ between the granting jurisdiction and the local government. Or the budget document may use different acronyms for the same grant source which makes it very difficult to aggregate.

The bottom part of Fig. 3.1 also includes employee contributions for pensions and OPEBs as well as special district revenues, typically user fees and charges. Cash management proceeds and fund transfers also contribute to General Fund revenues. These revenue sources are often not under the total control of the budget office because of either legal constraints or political pressures.

Contributions for Pensions and Other Post-Employment Benefits

These are funds, typically withheld from a local government employee's paycheck, that finance pensions and other post-employment benefits. This means that they are immediately earmarked for these purposes, although there is discretion as to what the benefits package that the employee receives will look like. Elected officials design the benefits package but pension fund governance typically resides with a separate legal entity, usually called the public employees retirement system (PERS). After the benefits package is determined, it is up to the PERS board to accumulate enough assets to pay for those benefits. This PERS Board invests the accumulated assets. About 70–75 percent of a pension system assets accumulate through the return on investments, with the rest coming from employee contributions. The PERS Board invests over a long-term time horizon and so can take some short-term risks (Peng, 2013). OPEBs consist primarily of health care costs. Until recently, there was little serious analysis of OPEBs. However, GASB statements 43 and 45 issued in 2004, forced local governments to calculate their costs. After this calculation, local governments found that these costs were a huge unfunded liability. This is causing local governments to attempt to contain these costs, prefund them, or issue bonds to fund them (Peng, 2013).

User Fees and Charges

Fees and charges make up about 20–30 percent of total revenues and have maintained this percentage over a long period.[9] They are based on the benefit principle of taxation—charge consumers for the benefits they receive. Of course, this assumes that consumers could opt out of receiving the benefits and therefore opt out of paying the charge. Correctly determined, meaning that they reflect the true cost of service provision, they link services provided with the demand for those services. If residents can opt out of paying by not using, concepts such as regressive, proportional, or progressive are irrelevant. However, in many cases, this ability to opt out is not available (sewage fees and water fees) and in these cases the fee is probably regressive.

A variety of services, including water, sewage disposal, parking, bridge tolls, highway tolls, garbage collection, and recreation use fees and charges as a part of their funding mechanism. Additionally, the criminal justice system extensively uses traffic and parking fines and court fees. In many of these examples, the local jurisdiction, typically using finance department analysis, establishes special districts to administer the fee and establish special funds within the budget to account for these fees. Budgets often include internal charges between departments, where, for example, the data processing department may charge other departments for their services. In some cases, fees and charges do not cover the full cost of the service provision and there needs to be a subsidy from the General Fund. If it is necessary to increase taxes to provide this subsidy, this is another example of expenditures driving the tax rate.

Because of tax limitations, new developments often do not pay their own way, in terms of generating enough revenue to cover the costs of

[9] Chapman (2013) or Hendrick (2013).

providing services. Impact fees, imposed on the developer, but perhaps shifted to the new residents can cover these costs. Based on a variety of bases, size of water pipes, drainage pipes, etc., these fees can add a good amount to the costs of development. Additionally, local governments may force developers to provide certain amenities (parks and bicycle paths) at the developers' expense. These exactions save the local jurisdiction money.

It is interesting that fees and charges have not generated an extensive analytic literature compared to property and sales taxes or intergovernmental revenue trends. However, they are important and generate a good deal of political discussion. Unfortunately, many texts give them short shrift.

Cash Management

Most of the time, local government revenues do not precisely match local government expenditures. This means that at times, local governments may have a cash surplus, which they can utilize to generate additional revenues. Proper management of this short-term money, almost always by the city treasurer, can generate revenues that flow into the General Fund. Typically, the treasurer uses this short-term cash for the buying and selling long-term and short-term debt.[10] It quickly can become a very complicated process and treasurers need to resist the temptation to make foolish investments. For example, the Orange County, California treasurer invested in some very esoteric bonds which ultimately led to a declaration of bankruptcy for Orange County.

Because of the amount of money and risk involved, state investment policy guidelines that emphasize safety, liquidity (how easy it is to get the money), and yield—in that order—control local cash management. Peng (2013) identifies six major components of any investment policy: what are allowable investments and what are not; maturity and liquidity constraints, credit risk, diversification, internal control, and reporting and oversight. To help local governments invest their funds, most states (and sometimes counties) have investment pools into which local governments can place short-term surpluses into a pool that the state or county

[10] In some jurisdictions, it may be possible to issue debt to raise revenues. Aside from capital projects or activities that generate a secure cash flow, this is a very risky behavior.

manages. These pools are conservatively managed so there is not much chance of losing the principle.

Cash management can be quite complex, with a variety of interest producing investments available for the jurisdiction to buy and sell. It is easy for the treasurer or finance director to feel pressure to produce large returns on the investments. This is especially true if the local government is running a short-term deficit and can use the extra money that the city treasurer can gain by taking risker choices when investing the idle funds.

Fund Transfers

Another revenue source, at least in some jurisdictions, is transfers from other funds into the General Fund. For example, if a city maintains a water service fee in a special fund, and if the water department makes a profit, some of this profit could well end up in the General Fund. The greater amount of these possibilities, the lower the sales and property tax rate can become.

As earlier noted, legal tax limits can significantly constrain local governments. The diversity of revenue sources reflects the impact of these limits. Today, most jurisdictions have learned to live within the limit constraints, but they are always present in budget deliberations. The finance department must be involved in the limit discussions because the budget reflects their impact.

Expenditures

Additionally, as Fig. 3.1 hypothesizes, local expenditures influence local revenues. As demand for public services increases, the governance system must either deny this demand, find expenditure cuts in other areas, or raise revenues. There is a two-way relationship between revenues and expenditures. An increase in revenues can lead to an increase in expenditures and an increase in expenditures can lead to an increase in revenues. This relationship sometimes leads to an overuse of dynamic capabilities as the leaders of the jurisdiction concoct ways of satisfying the new demands.

Bibliography

Arizona Tax Research Association. (2016 edition). *Arizona property taxes*. Phoenix. Retrieved March 26, 2021, from http://www.arizonatax.org/publication/books/explanation-arizona-property-taxes-2016-edition

Bergstrom, T. C., & Goodman, R. P. (1973, June). Private demands for public goods. *The American Economic Review, 63*(3), 280–296.

Brien, S. (2018). Compensating changes to the property tax levy? An empirical test of the residual rule. *Public Finance Review, 48*(6), 949–973.

Brooks, L., Halberstam, Y., & Phillips, J. (2016, June). Evidence from municipal fiscal constraints. *National Tax Journal, 69*(2), 315–322.

Chapman, J. (2013). Local government spending and revenues. In J. R. Bartle, W. B. Hildreth, & J. Marlowe (Eds.), *Management policies in local government finance* (6th ed., pp. 15–39). Washington, DC: International City/County Management Association.

Chapman, J. I. (1988). Land use planning and the local budget: A model of their interrelationships. *Public Administration Review, 48*(4), 800–806.

Chapman, J. I. (2008). The fiscalization of land use: The increasing use of innovative revenue raising instruments to finance public infrastructure. *Public Works Management and Policy, 12*(4), 551–567. State and local fiscal sustainability: The challenges. *Public Administration Review* (Special Issue), S115–S131.

Chernick, H. (2017). *Evaluating the effect of differences in revenue systems on the fiscal health of large U.S. cities* (Working Paper WP17HC1). Lincoln Institute of Land Policy.

Ellickson, R. C. (2020). *Zoning and the cost of housing: Evidence from silicon valley, greater New Haven, and greater Austin*, January 13, 2020. Available at SSRN. Retrieved June 2, 2021, from https://ssrn.com/abstract=3472145 or http://dx.doi.org/10.2139/ssrn.3472145

Felix, A. R. (2008). The growth and volatility of state tax revenue sources in the tenth district. *Federal Reserve Bank of Kansas City Economic Review*, 3rd Quarter, 63–88.

Hendrick, R. (2013). Nontax revenue. In J. R. Bartle, W. B. Hildreth, & J. Marlowe (Eds.), *Management policies in local government finance* (6th ed., pp. 219–250). International City/County Management Association.

Horiuchi, C., & Chapman, J. (2019). TIF in California: Birth, growth, death and re-birth(?) In C. L. Johnson & K. Kriz (Eds.), *Tax increment financing and economic development: Uses, structures and impact* (2nd ed., Chapter 9).

McCaffery, J. (Ed.). (1981). Special issue on the impact of resource scarcity on urban public finance. *Public Administration Review, 41*, 179–189.

Mikesell, J. L. (2013). Consumption and income taxes. In R. Bartle, W. B. Hildreth, & J. Marlowe (Eds.), *Management policies in local government finance* (6th ed., pp. 193–218). International City/County Management Association.

Mikesell, J. L. (2014). *Fiscal administration* (10th ed.) Wadsworth. Boston.

Mikesell, J. L. (2018, September/October). Often wrong, never uncertain: 40 years of state revenue forecasting. *Public Administration Review, 78*(5), 795–802.

Oates, W. (1972). *Fiscal federalism*. Harcourt Brace Jovanovich.

Oates, W. E., & Schwab, R. M. (1997). The impact of urban land taxation: The Pittsburgh experience. *National Tax Journal, 50*(1), 1–21.

Peng, J. (2013). Cash, investments, and pensions. In J. R. Bartle, W. B. Hildreth, & J. Marlowe (Eds.), *Management policies in local government finance* (6th ed., pp. 297–313). International City/County Management Association.

Randall, M., Gordon, T., Freene, S., & Erin, H. (2018). *Follow the money: How to track federal funding to local governments*. Urban Institute.

Ross, J. M. (2018, March). Fiscal zoning and fiscal externalities. *National Tax Journal, 71*(1), 45–74.

Smolka, M. (2012, June). A new look at value capture in Latin America. *Land Lines*. Lincoln Institute of Land Policy. https://www.lincolninst.edu/publications/articles/new-look-value-capture-latin-america

Wang, J., & Gorina, E. (2018). Fiscal effects of municipal annexation: Evidence from a large national sample of urban municipalities. *Growth and Change, 49*, 1–24.

Youngman, J. (2016). *A good tax*. Lincoln Institute of Land Policy.

CHAPTER 4

The Expenditure Module

Abstract This chapter analyzes the expenditure side of the budget, with an emphasis on expenditures rather than on services. It provides six explanations for expenditures: Baumol's Disease, availability of revenues, demographic changes, economic development projects, debt, and the governance system. It discusses the importance of governance decisions, intergovernmental mandates, and skinny budgets. It includes a discussion of the Tiebout model as well as macro-economic effects and the role of environmental justice of expenditure decisions. The chapter also presents a litany of interrelationships among the variables, including, for example, tax increment financing, tax and expenditure limitations, pensions, equity concerns, and the importance of the economic base of the jurisdiction.

Keywords Baumol Disease · Equity · Demographics · Governance

Cities collect revenue to finance service provision. Similar to the preceding chapter on revenues, this chapter will not discuss the internal budget processes of the jurisdiction but will focus on the complex set of interacting factors that influence the expenditure side of budget outcomes (see Fig. 4.1). Many of these factors interact with other factors. In the following discussion, the primary focus will be on expenditures rather

J. Chapman, *The Local Budget as a Complex System*,
Palgrave Studies in Public Debt, Spending, and Revenue,
https://doi.org/10.1007/978-3-030-94903-7_4

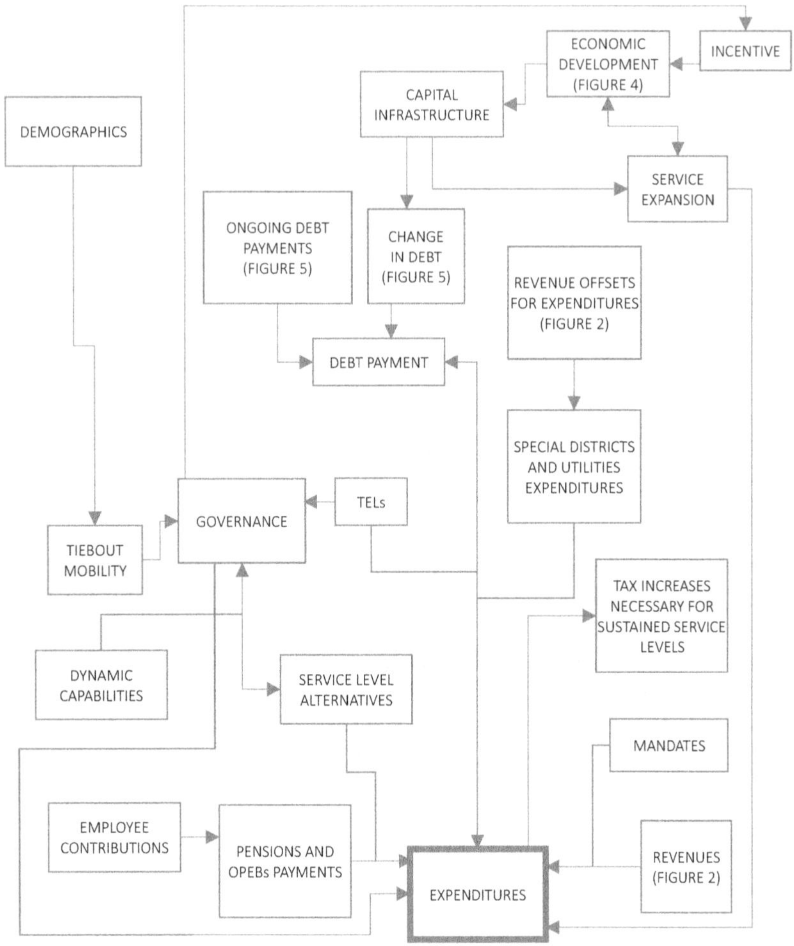

Fig. 4.1 Expenditures

than on service delivery. Obviously, there is a direct connection between how much a city spends on a particular service and the quantity of service delivered. However, different mechanisms of providing that service, as determined by the governance and dynamic capacity of the city might imply a different level of expenditures for the same amount of service delivered. Finally, there is some evidence that expenditure patterns for

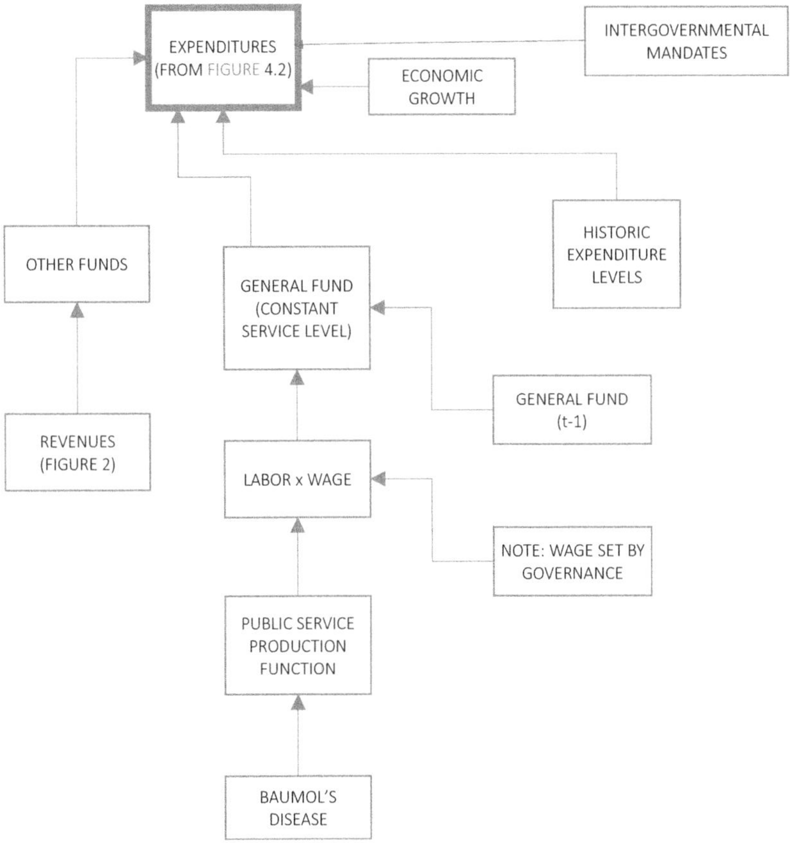

Fig. 4.2 Expenditures (continued)

cities usually do not greatly change over time. In 2006, municipalities spent about 16 percent of total expenditures on public safety and about 15.5 percent on the environment and housing. These are very similar to the 1991 percentages of 15.5 percent and 16 percent respectively (Chapman, 2013).

Like Figs. 3.1 and 3.2, Fig. 4.1 is presented in two discrete sections. There are too many variables that independently influence the expenditure patterns of the jurisdiction to be expressed in one diagram.[1] Further, because of the complexity of the expenditure decision-making, not all of the variables will be analyzed in this monograph.

The first factor is the demographic composition of the jurisdiction. The expectation is that cities with a large percentage of retired inhabitants would spend money on a different pattern of services than a city that was full of young families. Once this expenditure pattern is set (as Fig. 3 hypothesizes), it may be that the Tiebout Model (Tiebout, 1956) becomes a useful explanation for some of the revenue and expenditure decisions that the dynamic capabilities and governance factors indicate. The Tiebout Model, one of the best-known models in local government economics, argues that under a certain set of assumptions, people will move to the city that best meets their demands for a particular revenue–expenditure package. This overall sorting of potential residents will reinforce this package, and it may be possible that a population equilibrium among jurisdictions will occur, with multiple jurisdictions offering different budgetary packages. There seems to be some evidence that the Tiebout model has some validity (Fischel, 2006; Oates, 1969; Tabellini, 2018). Interestingly, there is also some evidence that this model might be applicable to other countries (Balestra et al., 2018). Notice that this is consistent with the exit, voice, and loyalty model of Hirschman (1970), but would focus on the exit component. To the extent that current residents are not satisfied with what their local government is doing, they also have the option, according to Hirschman, of speaking out against the government's decision, thereby using the voice option. A final example (Cornaggia et al., 2019) also seems to indicate that local government spending affects the income distribution in the jurisdiction through changes in local population composition and income distribution that arise from the population movements into and out of that jurisdiction. This is consistent with the Tiebout/Hirschman models.

An additional way that demography can influence expenditures is by examining the various elasticities associated with some of the major expenditure sources. Although the data is somewhat dated, the income elasticity for total local goods and services ranges from 0.34 to 0.89 (Inman,

[1] Figure 4.2 was divided into taxes and other revenue sources.

1979)—for a 10 percent increase in income, there will be an increase of 3.4–8.9 increase in demand for the public good or service. Thus, higher-income people demand more services.

The second factor affecting expenditures is that steadily increasing costs have also led to increasing local budgets. Baumol (1967) argued that most services provided by city governments are services in which productivity increases are difficult to achieve and thus this characteristic of the technology of producing these services prevents the offsetting of increased wages by technological improvements and therefore the unit costs of these services will rapidly increase. These increasing costs, sometimes referred to as "Baumol's Disease" were hypothesized to lead to an urban budgetary crisis. This crisis has not occurred because of stringent budget measures as well as TELs. Later, Bradford et al. (1969) find additional empirical work that indicates that rising unit costs are probably the most important source of increases in local public budgets.[2] Note that as Helland and Tabarrok (2019) show, even with productivity increases, not all prices fall because price is a relative measure so that the price of many public services has risen only relative to other goods.

The third factor is the availability of revenues. The previous chapter on revenues argued that the need for public services has an impact on the level of revenues of the jurisdiction. Here it is argued that the availability of revenues can lead to an increase in expenditures. If money is available, it is likely to be spent. Note that this is not inconsistent with the argument that expenditures are negatively related to the tax rate (Bergstrom & Goodman, 1973)—higher tax rates can lead to a decline in desired expenditures but still generate enough revenues to offset that decline. In the short run, if more than the forecasted revenues appear, they are often appropriated to a "rainy-day" fund for future expenditures or might be spent on one-time additions to services or the capital stock of the jurisdiction. Tax decreases seldom voluntarily occur. If tax rates are the price of services, the price elasticity of local goods and services ranges from −0.23 to −0.56, which indicates that as tax rates increase, the demand for services decreases (Inman, 1979).[3]

[2] However, Triplett and Bosworth (2003) find that there have been increases in the productivity of service industries, although they do not specifically study local budgets.

[3] There is some variation when particular services are examined. Police and fire elasticities range from −0.19 to −0.92; Parks and recreation range from −0.19 to −1.00 and Public Works ranges from −0.92 to −1.00 (Inman, 1979).

The fourth factor is economic development. Chapter 6 extensively treats this factor (see Fig. 6.1). Although sometimes ignored in the discussion of the budget, economic development projects usually involve an increase in infrastructure provision which involves both debt issuance and development costs. It also involves a need for service expansion in the newly developed (or redeveloped) area, for example, there will be a need for more public safety provision, more sanitation, and waste disposal. Further, to the extent that the city offers tax incentives to the developer, this might also affect expenditures if the development is successful. There are also state programs that authorize various economic development incentives, such as Tax Increment Financing and federal government programs, such as Opportunity Zones, that also impact the budget.

The fifth factor affecting expenditures is debt. Debt will also be extensively treated later in the monograph (see Fig. 5.1). In summary, jurisdictions issue debt for two reasons: to finance city improvements or to cover an excess of expenditures over revenues. This latter reason is almost always unacceptable, and this monograph will not discuss this activity. It is possible to fund capital and service projects by either pay-as-you-go financing which uses current incoming revenues that the project generates and which drive city expenditures or using debt financing, which depends on the availability of future debt service funds, which are determined by economic conditions, tax revenues and the willingness of the governance system to commit to meet the debt service requirements. Note that expenditures for debt by the jurisdiction are artificially low because the interest payment on municipal debt is usually tax-exempt (from both the national and state governments) and is thus below the market rate. This allows savings to the issuing jurisdiction and therefore lower expenditures. Depending upon the type of debt issued, debt management can be quite complex, depending upon the type of bonds issued (Denison, 2013).

The sixth factor influencing the level of expenditures is the type of governance environment that surrounds the budget. Governance in this sense involves several different aspects. The first is the measurement and determination of the service level. Using police as an example, the first step might be to determine what is the optimal level of crime in the jurisdiction. This optimal level is greater than zero (assuming diminishing returns to police inputs) because driving the crime rate to zero would be prohibitively expensive. Once the optimal level is determined, then the service level must be determined, for example, for police, is the service level measured by crime rates (or crime rate reduction) or by police per capita. Further, should the goal be a minimization of crimes over the entire city, the equalization of crime rates over all areas of the city or the equal distribution of police inputs over different areas of the city. Each of these alternatives has different expenditure ramifications.

A second component of governance would be the dynamic capability of the city. Some cities are just more innovative than others (Svara & Nelson, 2012). However, it is possible to teach some degree of innovation to city administrators and staff. The Innovation Academy at Arizona State University has had some success in increasing innovation capabilities in select cities and counties (Chapman, 2015), in particular, with extensive innovation training, participants found improved communications within the jurisdiction, improvements in organizational skills, and sometimes an improvement in the culture of the organization. An additional measure of the dynamic capability of the city would be its willingness to utilize many of the available tools that government could use. These tools include (among others) public–private bargains in forming partnerships (Kirlin & Kirlin, 1982), contracting out, and grants and loan guarantees (Salamon, 2002). All of these tools help local governments provide services at lower costs. The development and use of the tools reflect on the dynamic capabilities of the city.

A final component of governance is the political system of the jurisdiction. If city manager governments have different expenditure levels than strong mayor governments, then jurisdictions with conservative electorates are likely to have small governments and thus less revenues and expenditures than cities with a more liberal electorate. Another part of the pollical atmosphere is the relationship of the city to land use decisions. Some cities encourage development by making zoning less restrictive—more commercial and industrial zoning or more small lot size zoning. Less restrictive zoning should not only lead to more revenues, as noted in the last chapter, but also more expenditures.

Another expenditure determining variable is the extent of the constraints imposed by tax and expenditure limitations (TELs). While 33 states have some sort of tax and/or expenditure limit, they vary in their effectiveness, with citizen initiative enacted limits more effective in restraining the growth in government than legislative limits (Kallen, 2017). TELs may also have an impact of tax-supported debt. Kioko and Zhang (2019) found that if the limit applies to assessed property valuation or the property tax rate, the TEL has a negative impact on the use of tax-supported debt. Less studied are tax and expenditure limits that cities impose. Brooks and Phillips (2009) found that these local limits are prevalent but virtually impossible to identify by reading municipal charters and codes. Most also have override mechanisms. They found that about 40 percent of the officials of TEL-adopting cities reported that the TEL had no effect. However, about 20 percent of the cities did reduce service provision, that is potentially reduced expenditures, because of the TEL.

As the bottom section of Fig. 4.1 illustrates, there are a variety of other influences on local government expenditures. These are mostly exogenous to the internal budget deliberations of the jurisdiction.

The first influence to consider is how much discretion does the governance system have over determining the level of expenditures. There is little empirical research at the local level in this area; however, after a very detailed examination of a sample of state spending, Gordon et al. (2019) determined that some states faced restrictions on close to 90 percent of their total state spending, while other states faced restrictions on only 27 percent. At the federal level, Wildavsky and Caiden (2004) investigate the politics of the budgetary process, with some discussion of incrementalism. While no empirical data is available as to the percentage of the local budget in time (t) is dependent on the budget in ($t - 1$), it is reasonable to assume that major budget changes will not occur in the aggregate or even at a particular service level. This relationship probably holds most strongly for the General Fund and assumes that the General Fund is financing a constant service level. However, there are additional pressures on expenditures that might offset this variable and affect the level of expenditures.

A second influence would be that of governmental mandates. Mandates are requirements that local governments must undertake certain activities whether or not the mandate comes with financial assistance. They can be very broad (such as provision of health services as a condition for state or federal funding), or they can be very limited in merely describing how to undertake a particular task. These mandates often connect with the intergovernmental revenue flows discussed in Chapter 3 and direct how the jurisdiction must spend the grants. Sometimes these mandates are very convoluted, and sometimes they are straightforward. Sometimes local governments might ignore the mandates because of their belief that the risk of an audit is very low. This is usually not a good practice for the budget department. These mandates can come from several different funding agencies and may affect several different departments within the jurisdiction. There is even a chance that they may conflict.

A third source of expenditure decisions is both loosely tied to revenues and is mandated by law. These are expenditures on pensions and other post-employment benefits (OPEBs). Local governments sometimes have the option of joining a statewide investment pool for pensions (and thus face statewide rules for pension provision expenditures) or managing their own pension system. The majority of local pension assets are in statewide managed systems. There are two principal types of pension plans. Defined benefits plans guarantee a pension benefit at the time of retirement and which is set by formula. Most public sector benefit plans are of this type. The second type is a defined contribution plan, in which the employer makes a guaranteed payment into the pension fund, but the employee's benefits are not guaranteed. Defined benefit plans often generate large unfunded pension liabilities. This puts additional pressure on municipalities to increase their contributions, and thus expenditures. Mead (2013) identifies three cost containment plans: change features of the current defined benefit plan, switch from a defined benefit plan to a defined contribution plan, and a switch from a defined benefit plan to a hybrid plan. If the governance system changes current benefit plan features, it is important to remember that these changes can only apply to new hires since in most cases state constitutions, statutes, or the courts guarantee current employee benefits. Some suggestions for changing the plans include raising the retirement age or increasing employee contributions. Switching to a defined contribution plan seems to be politically unfeasible—only one city in the United States has done so. Hybrid plans tend to share the pension risks between the employee and the jurisdiction (both positive and negative risks). A final suggestion is for the jurisdiction to issue pension obligation bonds to payoff this unfunded liability, however, this method tends to be riskier because it assumes that the rate of investment return on the bonds is greater than the interest rate payments on the bonds. Pension obligation bonds will be further discussed in the debt chapter.

"Baumol's Disease" affects total expenditures through two components—labor and salary. First, as the local budget constraint becomes stricter, at a given wage level, there is some likelihood that the number of workers hired will fall. For example, local governments lost about 1,000,000 jobs between February and September 2020 (NACO, 2020), the height of the COVID-19 recession. But with fewer budget constraints, local employment should increase as service levels increase. During the 2011–2015 period, there was a difference that varied widely among the wages and benefits of federal civilian employees and those of similar private sector employees. The difference depended upon the level of education of the employee. Those federal workers with a bachelor's degree earned (including benefits) about 5 percent more than they would have in the private sector; those with a high school education earned about 34 percent more, while those with professional degrees or doctorates earned about 24 percent less (CBO, 2017).[4] The product of labor and wages determines about 80 percent of the expenditures of local governments.

A "skinny budget" focuses on the expenditure side of the document. The term may not mean a smaller budget than in the previous year but rather is smaller in the budget's documentation. It usually does not go into great deal of detail about the internal programmatic budgets but rather just gives the aggregate for the various programs. It does not necessarily set priorities, although by examining changes in the aggregates, it is certainly possible to discern any priority changes. This is the first step in the budget process because it forms a basis for budget negotiations. Skinny budgets tend to be very conservative in estimating revenues and expenditures. Figure 4.1 shows that the components of the skinny budget—historic expenditure levels and constant General Fund service levels, directly impact expenditure levels. Essentially, it is a bare-bones version of the budget, with the final budget document being much larger. While skinny budgets are rare at the city level, they are becoming more popular at the state level. Sometimes skinny budgets are so lean that it is difficult to determine how the expenditures will really change.

The macro-environment also has an impact on expenditure levels. There are two components to this environmental influence: the national economic component and the economic base of the city component.[5] The national component is the state of the national economic condition. If there is a growth slowdown or recession, then national economic growth will be less or even negative. To the extent that the jurisdiction feels this slowdown, it will find that revenues will fall and there will be

[4] Note that these are federal salary and benefits. Local governments vary a great deal and are difficult to generalize.

[5] The demographic influence on expenditures (which is also a macro component) has already been discussed.

pressure to reduce expenditures. However, simultaneously, there will be pressure to increase social services because there will be more unemployment. Unfortunately, the city has little impact on the national economic environment.

The economic base of the city also influences expenditures. For example, if it is a highly industrialized city, then to the extent that demand for the products produced remains static, the city can expect a calm environment. However, if the demand shifts, then the city could find itself having to change its expenditure levels. Note that these last two concepts are highly intertwined, but both refer to the fact that the city has little control over their changes but must respond to these exogenous influences. Of course, the reverse is also true. Cities prosper during good economic times and therefore can afford to increase expenditure levels and if the city economic base expands, that should also generate the ability to increase levels. Finally, as discussed earlier, the city may have the ability to encourage the development of a strong economic base, typically through its economic development activities (see Chapter 6) and its land use regulation discussion.

Another factor that exerts pressure on the level of expenditures is the governance system's concerns about equity. There are several dimensions to this topic. First, as earlier discussed, while there is a relationship between expenditures and service provision, this may not be a linear relationship and may vary by mode of provision. Doubling of expenditures might not mean a doubling of service output. Direct provision of a service by the jurisdiction may not lead to the same level of expenditures for the service if a public–private partnership provides the same level of service. For these concerns, the question becomes one of equity in the distribution of resources or final outputs. As the police example earlier in this chapter demonstrated, there are political judgments inherent in some very basic decisions.

Service delivery equity is also a function of both the dynamic capability of the city and the governance structure of the city. A jurisdiction with high levels of dynamic capability will recognize that there are multiple ways of providing a service, ranging from contracting out to public–private partnerships.[6] While state or federal legislation or mandates might circumscribe the use of some of these tools, there still might be some

[6] For a long list of these tools, see Salamon (2002).

mechanisms that would allow the same service level and a lower level of expenditures. The governance component will relate to the implementation of the ideas generated by the jurisdiction's dynamic capabilities. Politics may also hamstring an innovative and beneficial way of providing a service.

A final equity concern is the siting of unpleasant infrastructure. It is not unusual for governments to site such physical infrastructure as sewer plants or landfills next to the housing of the poor or non-white communities. Allowing the construction of major freeways through poor neighborhoods or allowing perverse zoning to occur (forbidding high-rise housing) are other examples. These are examples of the lack of environmental justice, and local decision-makers must always consider these issues when analyzing both capital and service expenditures.

In general, it sometimes appears that spending more money can fix these equity concerns. Unfortunately, this implies that increasing revenues is necessary, probably through tax increases, or alternatively through the reduction of service levels in other areas. This may be why local officials often ignore equity issues. However, this may be changing as society becomes more aware of these issues.[7]

Because of the many variables and their complex relationships that affect expenditures, it can be quite difficult to forecast future expenditure levels. In particular, the forecasts must include revenue forecasts, macroenvironmental forecasts, demographic forecasts, mandate forecasts, and governance forecasts.[8] It becomes particularly difficult to conceptualize since some of these variables may be exogenous to the model, at least in the short run. In particular, revenues, the macroeconomic climate, and demographics demonstrate this exogeneity. Therefore, the budget office must exercise extreme caution in generating multi-year expenditure forecasts. The office should also use prudence in examining expenditure trend lines generated by regression techniques since expenditure policies are malleable. However, for some components of total expenditures, notably pensions and OPEBs, the forecasts can be quite accurate because these depend on current employment.

[7] See Campbell et al. (2015).

[8] This analysis does not address forecasting court decisions which also can have a major impact on expenditures.

Bibliography

Balestra, C., Boarini, R., & Tosetto, E. (2018). *What matters the most to people? Evidence from the OECD better life Index users responses* (OECD Statistics Working Papers. 2018/03). OECD Publishing. Retrieved August 21, 2019, from https://doi.org/10.1787/edf9a89a-en

Baumol, W. J. (1967, June). Macroeconomics of unbalanced growth: The anatomy of urban crises. *American Economic Review, 57*, 415–426.

Bergstrom, T. C., & Goodman, R. P. (1973, June). Private demands for public goods. *The American Economic Review, 63*(3), 280–296.

Bradford, D. F., Malt, R. A., & Oates, W. E. (1969, June). The rising cost of local public services: Some evidence and reflections. *National Tax Journal, XXII*(2), 185–202.

Brooks, L., & Phillips, J. (2009, April). Municipally imposed tax and expenditure limits (pp. 8–13). *Land Lines*. Lincoln Institute of Land Policy.

Campbell, H. E., Eckerd, A. M., & Kim, Y. (2015). *Rethinking environmental justice in sustainable cities: Insights from agent-based modeling*. Routledge

Chapman, J. (2013). Local government spending and revenues. In J. R. Bartle, W. B. Hildreth, & J. Marlowe (Eds.), *Management policies in local government finance* (6th ed., pp. 15–39). International City/County Management Association.

Chapman, J. (2015, October). *Innovation academy evaluation (2013–2015) for the alliance for innovation*. Arizona State.

Congressional Budget Office. (2017, April). *Comparing the compensation of federal and private-sector employees 2011 to 2015*. 52637-federalprivatepay.pdf. Accessed 14 Apr 2021.

Cornaggia, J., & Gustafson, M., Israelsen, R. D., & Ye, Z. (2019, August 13). Government spending and local demographics: Evidence from Moody's municipal Ratings recalibration. Retrieved August 29, 2019, from https://ssrn.com/abstract=3437023

Denison, D. (2013). Debt management. In J. R. Bartle, W. B. Hildreth, & J. Marlow (Eds.), *Management policies in local government finance* (6th ed., pp. 279–295). International City/County Management Association.

Fischel, W. A. (Ed.). (2006). *The Tiebout model at 50*. Lincoln Institute of Land Policy.

Gordon, T., Randall, M., Steuerle, E., & Boddupalli, A. (2019, July). *Fiscal democracy in the states*. Urban Institute.

Helland, E., & Tabarrok, A. (2019). *Why are the prices so damn high?* George Mason University.

Hirschman, A. O. (1970). *Exit, voice, and loyalty: Responses to decline in firms, organizations, and states*. Harvard University Press.

Inman, R. (1979). The fiscal performance of local governments. In P. Mieszkowski & M. Straszheim (Eds.), *Current issues in urban economics* (pp. 270–321). Johns Hopkins University Press.

Kallen, C. (2017, September). *State tax expenditure limitation and supermajority requirement: New and updated data* (AEI Economics Working Paper 2017–19). Retrieved April 8, 2021.

Kioko, S., & Zhang, P. (2019, March). Impact of tax and expenditure limits on local government use of tax-supported debt. *Public Finance Review, 47*(2), 409–432.

Kirlin, J. J., & Kirlin, A. M. (1982). *Public choices—Private resources.* California Tax Foundation.

Mead, D. M. (2013). Accounting and financial reporting. In J. R. Bartle, W. B. Hildreth, & J. Marlowe (Eds.), *Management policies in local government finance* (pp. 93–116). International City/County Management Association.

National Association of Counties. (2020, September 4). *Local government employment continues slump for fifth consecutive month.* Retrieved April 14, 2021, from https://www.naco.org/resources/featured/aug-jobs-report

Oates, W. (1969). The effects of property taxes and local public spending on property values: An empirical examination PF tax capitalization and the Tiebout hypothesis. *Journal of Political Economy, 77*, 957–971.

Salamon, L. M. (2002). *The tools of government.* Oxford University Press.

Svara, J. A., & Nelson, K. (2012). Form of government still matters: Fostering innovation in U.S. municipal governments. *American Review of Public Administration, 42*(3), 257–281.

Tabellini, M. (2018). *Racial heterogeneity and local government finances: Evidence from the great migration* (Harvard Business School Working Paper 19-006).

Triplett, J. E., & Bosworth, B. P. (2003, September). Productivity measurement issues in service industries: "Baumol's Disease" has been cured. *Federal Reserve Bank of New York Economic Policy Review*, 23–33. Retrieve April 7, 2021.

Tiebout, C. M. (1956). A pure theory of local expenditures. *Journal of Political Economy, 64*(5), 416–424.

Wildavsky, A., & Caiden, N. (2004). *New politics of the budgetary process.* Pearson.

CHAPTER 5

Debt

Abstract Although the city treasurer rather than the budget officer is primarily responsible for debt activities, these actions can have an influence on the budget. This chapter is a basic discussion of debt and its influences. It first argues for the development of a capital improvements plan before any debt is discussed. It then distinguishes between pay-as-you-go finance and debt finance, both of which have budget implications. The chapter then identifies five basic debt issues for the local government to consider: taxable versus tax-exempt debt, how much debt has the jurisdiction already issued, should the debt be sold in a competitive or non-competitive manner, what should be the structure of the debt, and the possibility for arbitrage. The chapter identifies four basic types of debts as well as several more narrowly defined types. It then distinguishes between short-term and long-term debts. It concludes by identifying several debt actors with whom the budget office will be interacting.

Keywords Bonds · Key participants · Debt types

For a detailed explanation of many of the topics discussed below, see California Debt and Investment Advisory Commission (2019) (CDIAC).

J. Chapman, *The Local Budget as a Complex System*,
Palgrave Studies in Public Debt, Spending, and Revenue,
https://doi.org/10.1007/978-3-030-94903-7_5

The capital budget often involves decisions concerning debt finance. This usually means that the city treasurer, not the budget officer, is responsible for the choice of the debt instrument and the administration of debt. However, since the city budget must include payments for debt service, it is reasonable to include debt as an influence on fiscal sustainability. Additionally, the choice and structuring of debt reflect both the complexity of local finance and the management capabilities of the local finance team.

Before the determination of the budgetary implications of debt, it is highly recommended that the local government develop a capital improvement plan. This involves the identification of all capital projects that the city is planning, the prioritization of these capital projects, and a stipulation of the expected completion dates of the projects. Part of this plan should include a section on the financing of the project. Of necessity, at a minimum, this involves consultation with the department managers of economic development, public health and safety, recreation, and transportation. Obviously, careful evaluation of wish list projects is necessary. After the completion of this evaluation, the jurisdiction must assess its ability to finance the desired amount, so forecasting future revenues and expenditures must occur. Finally, this is the time to take into account any legal constraints on the use of debt (Bunch, 2013). These often vary by state. There are also federal constraints, and how to work within these constraints often involves the dynamic capabilities of the local government to determine how to best finance the project.

After the capital needs are determined, the total debt expenditures can be examined. Figure 5.1 shows some of the influences on this determination. Note that Fig. 5.1 is an analysis of the debt environment assuming that the capital improvement plan has been accepted.

Once the jurisdiction decides what should be the necessary infrastructure, there are two ways of financing the new capital.[1] The first is "pay-as-you-go" (PAYGO) financing while the second is debt—sometimes referred to as "Pay-as-you-use." It is possible to make arguments for both techniques (Horler, 1987). For PAYGO, the arguments include:

[1] Cities also must ensure that there are adequate funds to cover the depreciation of infrastructure.

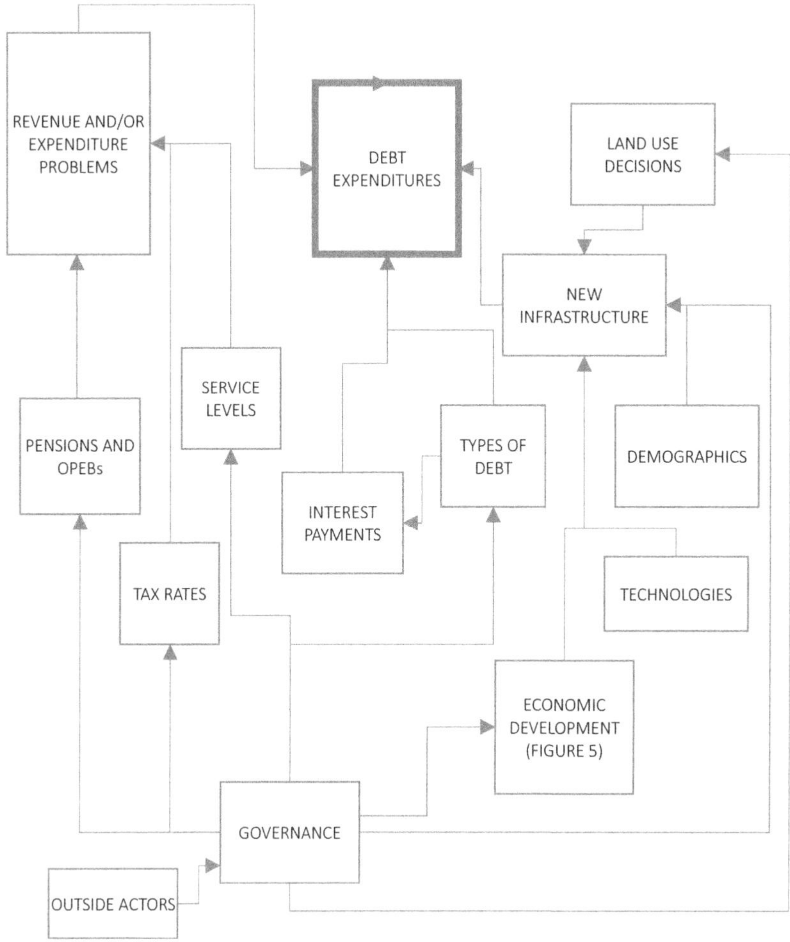

Fig. 5.1 Debt

- Since current residents are making the decision on the infrastructure, they should pay the costs, rather than future residents who have no say in the infrastructure's provision.
- There are no interest costs that arise from debt financing;
- There is a greater legacy of fully paid for infrastructure for future residents to enjoy.

Use debt financing when:

- The local government has limited funds from current revenues to support needed infrastructure.
- It is possible to schedule the debt repayment costs to fit the local government's revenue flows.
- With low interest rates on the debt (in part possible because of the federal tax exemption), it is possible to finance capital projects at low costs.
- It is possible to schedule the payment of the debt costs to match the benefits and/or useful life of the project.[2]

Some authors argue that the PAYGO method is the cheaper way to finance infrastructure because of the lack of interest payments (Horler, 1987). However, if the present value of the payments, including interest payments, is equal to the total cost of the project, there may be no difference in total financing costs. Nevertheless, it does entail a long-run commitment of revenues, which may limit the local government's ability to meet future unanticipated needs. It also will tend to slow down the development of the project. Debt does provide the opportunity to start projects sooner, complete them sooner, and therefore generate benefits sooner. Depending upon the community's fiscal circumstances, the local government might use both methods in combination. It is important to remember that, except in unusual or very specific circumstances, jurisdictions should not use debt to finance the difference between current expenditures and revenues. This is a deferral of financial responsibility and perhaps budget trickery, rather than a way of ensuring long-run fiscal sustainability.

While there are many concerns when debt is issued and there are a great number of technical processes to be aware of, there are five basic debt matters that the local government should consider. The first is to decide whether the debt should be taxable or tax-exempt at the federal level. Nearly all municipal debt issued is non-taxable.[3] This means that

[2] In very limited cases, there may be some legal arbitrage that can occur when interest costs of the debt are very low because of the tax-exempt status of the debt.

[3] In some cases, taxable bonds are an alternative for local governments. In this case, some restrictions in federal regulations can be ignored and in restrictions on service charges with private users (Horler, 1987).

the interest payment on the debt is usually lower than the market rate on taxable debt. This saves the jurisdiction money. It also makes the debt a valuable addition to the investment portfolio of the wealthy. A second concern is how much debt the jurisdiction has already issued as well as how much debt that overlapping jurisdictions have issued. The greater the debt already issued by the jurisdiction, the riskier new debt becomes and therefore a higher interest rate will be necessary for the debt to sell. Further, if other jurisdictions, for example, school districts, have issued debt using the same tax base, the households whose property is the basis for the debt payment, may object. There can also be special districts and community facilities districts that can issue debt that overlaps with the other jurisdictions. Too much overlapping debt can cause not only high tax rates for the debt service but also high-interest payments on the new debt. A third issue is whether to sell the debt in a competitive or non-competitive fashion.[4] The authorizing regulations usually determine the method of sale, but in some cases, the local government is free to decide. Over time, as the debt instruments become more complex, negotiated sales become more popular. In deciding if a sale should be negotiated or competitive, the local government should concern itself with the financing structure and the lowest cost of borrowing. Both competitive and negotiated sales involve many actors. Later in the chapter, there will be a discussion of the roles of some of these actors. Again, the dynamic capabilities of the local government come into play at this point because of the complexities of these decisions as well as the interactions with these actors. The fourth issue is the structure of the debt. Retirement of the bonds occurs in sections,[5] not all at once. How large is the size of each section determines the bonds' structure (as well as its interest rate). The maturity of the bond is the length of time for the payoff of the bond and bonds with longer maturity having to pay a different rate of interest (usually higher) than bonds with a short maturity, Additionally, the jurisdiction must be aware of different ways of calculating interest (for budgetary purposes). The competing ways are net interest costs and true interest costs, with true interest costs taking into account the time value of the

[4] Except in rare cases (typically private placement bonds), the local government does not sell debt directly to the public. Rather it uses an underwrite to do this. The local governments negotiate a price with the underwriter, or they use the market to competitively determine the price.

[5] Sometimes called "tranches."

payments. The fifth issue arises when the proceeds of the bond's sale do not match up with the expenditures on the projects that the bonds are financing. There may be a great deal of money sitting in the treasurer's office that the treasurer can invest (subject to severe arbitrage restrictions) in other finance instruments, with the resulting cash flow going into the General Fund. While this cash flow may be of great benefit to the city, the local budget must not be too dependent on these flows. Additionally, the jurisdiction must carefully monitor the type of investments of the debt proceeds that the treasurer makes. The Orange County bankruptcy, in part, occurred because the county was overly dependent on these flows and the treasurer was speculating in his investment of the debt proceeds.

Types of Debt

There are four basic categories of debt: General Obligation (GO) bonds, revenue bonds, assessment bonds, and conduit revenue bonds.[6] A General Obligation bond has its repayment guaranteed by the total revenue of the jurisdiction. It is not supported by the revenue from a particular project but by the full faith and credit of the issuing agency. From the buyer's point of view, GO bonds are the most secure because voters have authorized the issuer of the bond to levy a property tax on all properties within the jurisdiction at any rate necessary to raise enough money to service the debt. Because they are the most secure, GO bonds usually pay the lowest rate of interest. However, GO bonds face two significant constraints. The first is that in many cases, the state has set a limit to the amount of GO debt available. Since these limits are often constitutional, they bind the jurisdiction. The second difficulty is that issuing a GO bond almost always needs a successful vote by the electorate for their issuance. Extensive voter education is necessary for this to occur. The implication for the budget is that this GO rate becomes the base property tax rate—any property taxes necessary to finance city services are on top of this rate, which is a political constraint on the budget. This

[6] Pension obligation bonds are an added type that will be discussed later. There are several additional types of debt, for example, Certificates of Participation, that are available for use by the jurisdiction.

situation will sorely test the dynamic capabilities of the governance system (Denison, 2013).[7]

The second type of municipal debt is a revenue bond. This debt is backed by dedicated fees or earmarked sources of revenues, for example, highway tolls or user fees. They are far more popular than GO, although they too may need voter approval. These types of debt are usually not constrained by the state. One particular type of revenue bond is a lease-backed bond. The proceeds of the sale of these bonds finance the construction of government buildings, schools, or jails. These bonds are issued by a separate financing authority which then takes the money and finances the construction or purchase of the asset. The separate agency then leases the asset back to the government, the financing agency keeps title to the asset while the government makes lease payments that cover the debt service requirements. The lease typically matches the maturity of the bond, so that when the bond matures and the lease ends, the ownership of the asset transfers to the government. Lease-backed debt does not count against the statutory debt limits on GO debt and typically carries a higher interest rate (Denison, 2013).

Assessment bonds are among the oldest methods of financing public works, appearing in Roman law with the first documented use in the thirteenth century (Horler, 1987). Special assessment bond practices vary among states and sometimes among cities within the same state. Horler (1987) identifies four principles that are common to all special assessment procedures. First, the money raised from the special assessment bond must be used for a public purpose. The capital improvement must give a benefit to a well-defined and limited area of land. Second, the total assessment must not exceed the cost of the improvement and bond financing. Third, the amount of assessment on an individual parcel must be proportional to the benefit that a particular parcel receives. Fourth, the owner of the assessed land, by law, has an opportunity to object to the assessment. The uses of special assessments are varied: examples include street paving, sidewalks, curbs, gutters, sewers, water supply, street lighting, Off-street parking, landscaping, storm drainage systems, fire protection, retaining walls, and land stabilization. The interest rate of the bonds will vary by the security of the bonds, which depends on a variety of factors, including

[7] Limited obligation bonds are backed by a specified amount of revenues received from any local source, including property and sales taxes. If these funds are insufficient, the local government may pay from other funds.

growth patterns of the area, the size of the parcels and number of property owners, zoning of the property, land use, terrain, and topography. Cities, counties, and special districts often rely on this type of debt finance. It is possible to use a PAYGO system to finance many of the above examples. However, this would tap the General Fund and so by using assessment financing, the jurisdiction saves money, at least in the short run and the budget is less constrained.

The fourth type of bond is a conduit revenue bond. This is a category of bond that exists because of provisions of the Internal Revenue code of the federal government. These bonds finance projects for non-governmental borrowing and must satisfy the requirements of the IRS for tax-exempt private activity bonds. They may be issued by local governments. Often used for economic development or redevelopment projects, these bonds can have multiple impacts on the budget through the projects that they finance. Since the federal government authorizes this method of debt finance, local governments must carefully monitor tax legislative changes that occur at the national level. Conduit bonds primarily finance the following activities: infrastructure qualifying as exempt facilities such as transportation facilities (airports, mass commuting, and intercity rail facilities), utility facilities for water supply, sewage, solid waste disposal, and sometimes electricity and gas. The bond's proceeds can also help finance small manufacturing facilities (sometimes called Industrial Development Bonds),[8] hospitals, and other non-profit health care facilities, educational facilities, and multi-family housing developments serving low-income tenants (CDIAC, 2019).

The financial flows under a conduit revenue bond can be complex. The local government issues the bonds (with only a public hearing and without a public vote). The bond proceeds are loaned to a private developer. The private developer then makes loan repayments that match the bond's debt service. These loan payments are the revenues securing the bonds and the city must pay the debt service on the bonds only to the extent that it receives these payments. In practice, the private borrower makes payments directly to the trustee (CDIAC, 2019). There are typically volume caps on the issuance of these bonds and states may institute an allocation committee at the state level for this allocation.

[8] This type of debt is heavily circumscribed by federal and state laws, so legal consul is necessary.

Conduit revenue bonds do not involve the direct credit of the local government and because they are for projects usually not owned or operated by the local government, they sometimes have unique policy issues and therefore unique guidelines. These guidelines may vary from city to city, but most of them cover two areas—credit quality and the public benefits of the project. For credit quality, many jurisdictions require a minimum rating of at least "A" for any conduit issue (CDIAC, 2019). If they do not have this minimum rating, they must have a major public benefit, or they could be privately placed with sophisticated investors. The reason for demanding a minimum credit rating even though the local government has no legal liability to make the debt service payments is that the local government may believe that its fiscal reputation will be affected if the issue goes into default, even though the default is not the fault of the local government. There is also a chance that there will be litigation, and therefore potential litigation costs for the local government if there is a default. A second criterion is that the financed project meets the socially desirable goals of the jurisdiction. For example, some issuers require that the project will create jobs, provide affordable housing, or assist the community in other ways. Consideration of environmental benefits and costs must also occur. Projects financed by conduit bonds are often controversial; so the finance departments (both budget officer and treasurer) must carefully scrutinize this form of debt.

There is a myriad of other widely used types of debt instruments, all of which may have budget implications. A first example is a debt used to finance a Community Facilities District. First initiated in either California or Florida (there is some debate on the timing) in 1982, this type of debt allows cities, counties, special districts, school districts, and other forms of local government to form a separate district to finance certain types of public works through PAYGO, the sale of bonds, certain public services on a PAYGO basis, or any combination of these techniques (Horler, 1987). While the approval of a Community Facilities District may vary by state, it often includes a report that identifies which pieces of infrastructure or what services the Community Facilities District will finance. Then the jurisdiction develops an assessment procedure to payoff the bonds or finance the services. Finally, there is a vote of the landowners to establish the district. This method of financing is very useful for development projects because typically there are few landowners to vote on the establishment of the district. It is also useful for growing cities because the use of facilities districts to finance such services as libraries, parks, or police and fire services removes the necessity of financing these activities from the city budget. Residents are notified of their tax liability as they move into the district. This liability will change as the bonds are retired, services increased, or some combination of both. These districts are designed as a budget saving mechanism and are becoming popular in rapidly growing jurisdictions.

Every pension fund has an Unfunded Actuarial Accrued Liability (UAAL). This is the actuarial present value of all the funds' assets minus the actuarial present value of all future accrued liabilities. This calculation may be negative (indicating an over-funded UAAL) or positive (indicating an underfunded UAAL). This is not an accounting liability but rather an actuarial liability and it assumes that the current plan will continue in the future. The UAAL includes expected pay increases of the current members and expected future service costs for those members. Retirement benefit increases also affect the UAAL, as well as actuarial gains and losses. The jurisdiction may issue Pension Obligation bonds (POBs) to pay some or all this UAAL. Once sold, the bond's proceeds are transferred to the issuer's pension system as a prepayment of all or part of the unfunded liabilities and the pension board directs that the proceeds of the sale should be invested in the stock market or bond market. For this plan to succeed and give budget relief, the invested bond proceeds must earn a rate of return higher than the total cost of borrowing. If this is true, then this transaction reduces the annual pension contribution needed to fund the existing plan by more than the cost of borrowing. The payment of the debt service on POBs is usually an unconditional obligation of the issuer with the payment coming from the General Fund, potentially affecting the budget. The issuing jurisdiction must consider several policy concerns before issuing POBs. First, POBs are typically issued during periods of low taxable interest rates.[9] The assumption is that the economic benefit to the issuer is the spread between the interest rate on the bonds and the assumed rate of return on investments. There is no guarantee that this will automatically occur. Market turndowns can cause the UAAL to rise to the pre-POB level, Second, the UAAL is just a snapshot at a specific time. The jurisdiction can add new benefits, and other changing economic factors can affect the underlying actual assumptions. Issuing a POB does not eliminate this risk (CDIAC, 2019). Further, issuing POBs to fund

[9] Interest on POBs is not federally tax exempt (CDIAC, 2019).

annual pension contributions can have a negative impact on the issuer's credit rating. This is especially true if projected returns become lower than expected and the issuer needs to both service the POB debt and increase contributions. Additionally, if the lump sum prepayment occurs when reinvestment rates of return are relatively low, this may be disadvantageous to the issuer. Finally, the issuer typically authorizes POBs by resolution. This means that the issuer can bury the bonds in the budget document and the bonds will receive little or no public scrutiny.

Tax increment financing (TIF) is a common redevelopment (or development) tool that exists in 48 states.[10] While discussed in more detail in the economic development chapter, this section analyzes some of its debt components. It is similar to a conduit bond in that it helps private developers construct infrastructure. While details of each state's ability to use TIF may vary by state, in general they have the following similar characteristics. First, the local jurisdiction—whether city or county—establishes a redevelopment agency. The redevelopment agency has the power to issue bonds. The bond issuance does not need a public vote. The proceeds of the bonds can be used to acquire and develop real property, the construction of streets, sidewalks, highways, and the installation of public utilities if the purpose of the project is the redevelopment of blighted areas within the city's jurisdiction. Generally, the agency itself cannot construct or finance the construction of buildings, rather it must sell or lease the property for private development. The bonds are often referred to as tax allocation bonds. This is because the redevelopment agency can service the bonds by collecting the portion of the ad valorem taxes on the property that exceed the tax collections at the time of approval of the redevelopment plan. This added portion is the tax increment or tax allocation. Historically, there are four basic problems with TIF: redevelopment plans may have exceedingly long duration; blight is so loosely defined that the plan redevelops areas that are clearly non-blighted; the bond proceeds act as a competitive tool to attract development from other jurisdictions; and often there is displacement of the low-income population because of the plan's unwillingness to generate or rehabilitate low and moderate housing. There is also the question of whether the state will backfill the lost revenues to any overlapping jurisdictions. Because it is so easy to implement and appears to

[10] Arizona does not allow tax increment financing; California eliminated tax increment finance and replaced it with a modification of infrastructure financing districts.

be totally self-financing, it is very popular. However, for many it appears to be a give-away to wealthy developers, it forces low-income residents out of the area, and hurts overlapping jurisdictions that were property tax dependent, which may force the state to backfill the lost revenue. In California, the state's backfill to school districts became so large that the state eliminated the ability to use the TIF mechanism and replaced it with a different mechanism: An Enhanced Infrastructure Financing District (Horiuchi & Chapman, 2019; Seufert, 2015).

Short-term financing techniques also include a variety of debt instruments.[11] All of these techniques face legal restrictions as to size and use with their use declining over the last several years. Many of these techniques have budget implications. Jurisdictions use Bond anticipation notes (BANs) to ensure financing for a project which has bond issuance authorization, but the bonds have yet to be issued. BANs allow debt issuance in increments as the project progresses but before the bond proceeds are available. The security for BANs is the bond proceeds and revenues generated by the project. The legal basis for issuing BANs resides in various authorizing statutes of both the city and the state. A second short-term financing instrument is a grant anticipation note (GAN). These can be issued to eliminate a cash-flow deficit when there is a secured federal or state grant or loan. There are often significant requirements for the awarding of these grants or loans and therefore there is less uncertainty about the security of the grant. This makes the GAN easier to sell. The cash-flow deficit that the GAN covers usually results from a delay in the receipts of reimbursement for grant-eligible expenses.

A third type of short-term financing is a tax and revenue anticipation note (TRAN). Trans are issued by local governments to fund a cash-flow deficit in a fiscal year, typically they are issued at the beginning of the fiscal year and have a maturity of less than one year (CDIAC, 2019). Since some TRANs have a maturity greater than one year (up to three), they can be issued in one year and mature in another. They appear as a fund liability in the fund that is receiving the proceeds. They are used for many purposes, including current expenses, capital expenditures, repayment of indebtedness and investment, and reinvestment. The proceeds are usually deposited in the General Fund. Local governments usually

[11] Short term is less than three years.

use TRANs as a cash management tool that enables the local government to maintain expenditure outlays in an even manner even though it receives revenues such as property taxes on an uneven basis throughout the year. TRANs smooth the city's cash flow. Again, there is a myriad of constraints facing the issuance of TRANs, many designed to ensure that they are used to even out the flow rather than hide a structural deficit or to ensure that they are not being used for arbitrage since these pay a low interest rate compared to other investment opportunities, TRANs can be authorized by a resolution of the city council adopted in the fiscal year prior to the fiscal year in which the TRAN will be issued. No voter approval is necessary.

Debt Actors[12]

In addition to the budget department, there are many people (and organizations) that are involved in the municipal debt process. Some directly influence the local budget; others influence the budget only indirectly. The staff of the budget office must be aware of the actors because of their political influence or ability to influence steps in the debt issuing process, so it is worthwhile to have a quick capsule look at some of these participants.[13]

1. The city treasurer represents the city that is issuing the debt. The treasurer must first ensure that the bond is legal and meets the tax exemption requirements under the law. The treasurer oversees the selection of the debt financing team, including the bond counsel and either a financial advisor or both. The city treasurer and finance office select the team through a request for proposal process, reputations, relationships with the city, or recommendations from other cities. The composition of the team is based on several factors, including the type of debt issued, the procedural requirements for that type of debt, and the level of in-house sophistication of the city (CDIAC, 2019). The treasurer, representing the city,

[12] Much of the following material is abstracted from CDIAC (2019).

[13] There are many more that this monograph does not discuss. See CDIAC (2019) for a more complete identification and discussion.

then works with the team to issue debt to finance the infrastructure. The treasure and staff are responsible for reviewing all aspects of the financing plan, including all documents and, if there is any legal action, they must be prepared to defend the debt issuance.

2. The bond counsel is the attorney that gives legal opinions that the bonds are binding obligations of the city and the interest on the bonds is exempt from federal and state income taxes. This tax exemption statement is a very crucial part of the bond opinion. The bond opinion is not a financial recommendation as to the acceptability of the bond for the investor, but rather an opinion on the legality of the bonds. Often, the bond counsel is part of a legal team for an issue. The bond counsel may not be the underwriter's counsel.
3. The financial advisor is a professional consultant, often hired by the city through the office of the city treasurer, to give advice on the debt financing plan. The advisor may be a consulting firm, an investment banking firm or a commercial bank, The advisor typically reviews the financial feasibility of the project, assesses the revenue stream that will finance the debt service, recommends the financing structure of the debt, recommends a maturity schedule, prepares, on the city's behalf, the official statement for the underwriters and investors, and recommends the timing of the sale of the bonds, along with a variety of other duties. The financial advisor can only buy competitively sold bonds and even then, only in the secondary market.
4. The underwriter purchases the bonds from the city and then resells the bonds to investors. Often the underwriter forms a syndicate with other firms to minimize the selling risk that the underwriters face. If the sale is a negotiated sale, the jurisdiction selects the underwriter and syndicate teams early in the process and the underwriter may perform many of the financial advisor's services, including the method of financing and the debt's structure. In these cases, it is not unusual for the underwriter to hire an underwriter's counsel. In a negotiated sale, the underwriter mails the official statement to potential buyers, assesses the market conditions to recommend the pricing and timing of the sale, as well as some other disclosure duties. Also in a negotiated sale, the underwriter can engage in preselling the bonds, thereby lowering the risk and perhaps lowering the compensation for undertaking the risk. In a competitive sale,

underwriters compete and deliver sealed bids to the city and the city selects the underwriter that offers the best terms at that time. In both negotiated and competitive sales, compensation for the underwriters is the difference between what they pay for the bonds and how much investors will pay for the bonds when the underwriter resells them. There is generally a prohibition against underwriters doing business with the city if they have made political contributions to elected officials of the city.

5. The underwriter chooses the underwriter's counsel (who cannot be the same individual or firm as the bond counsel) to represent the underwriter's interests in a negotiated sale.[14] The underwriter's counsel reviews the documents prepared by the bond counsel and coordinates the preparation of the Official Statement. The underwriter's counsel provides a due diligence review to ensure that the city government, has enough security for the issue so that an investor can make a knowledgeable decision as to whether to buy. The underwriter pays the underwriter's counsel.
6. Credit rating agencies analyze the likelihood of the debt returning all the principal to the investor. That means that the credit rating is an opinion of the investment quality of the bond. Local government bond ratings are based on the general state of the economy (both state and national), the basis for the debt service, and the issuer's investment strategy. The issuer usually pays the rating agency with the compensation based on all the supporting documents provided by the financial advisor or underwriter. Some buyers of the debt face legal restrictions and must buy securities at or above specified credit ratings. Typically, investors demand a higher interest rate if the bonds are lower rated. Some finance professionals argue that the credit rating is the most important factor in determining the interest rate on bonds at a particular time (CDIAC, 2019). Even though bonds may not always face legal requirements for obtaining a rating, in most cases local governments find that unrated bonds are difficult to sell. This means that the buyer will demand a higher interest rate and therefore the jurisdiction will have added expenses. There are often periodic reviews of ratings, and they may be either upgraded

[14] Competitive sales usually do not need an underwriter's counsel.

or downgraded, so rating agencies expect periodic financial reports from the issuer.

7. Local government picks the trustee to perform one or more of the administrative duties relating to the bond. The trustee is usually a commercial bank or trust company. There are many potential duties of a trustee including holding the funds relating to a bond issue, maintaining a list of names and addresses of bond owners, paying interest on the bonds to the registered owners, paying the principal of the bonds to these owners upon maturity, disseminating annual reports, and mailing required notices to bondholders. The same trustee does not have to perform all these functions.

There are many other actors associated with debt, including credit enhancement providers, non-governmental borrowers, retail and institutional investors, and investment advisors. Many of these actors seem separated from the budget process; however, to the extent that they affect the cost of debt, they act as additional complexity variables as the jurisdiction strives for fiscal sustainability. Additionally, the opportunity for dynamic capabilities to reduce budget stress is clearly present in virtually all these positions.

Although the local government treasurer has duties distinct from the budget officer, the activities of the two are not only interrelated but add complexity to the budget process. Further, it is often in this arena that the jurisdiction can demonstrate its management capacities.

Bibliography

Bunch, B. (2013). Capital planning and budgeting. In J. R. Bartle, W. B. Hildreth, & J. Marlowe (Eds.), *Management policies in local government finance* (6th ed., pp. 253–278). International City/County Management Association.

California Debt and Investment Advisory Commission. (2019). *California debt financing guide*. California Debt and Investment Advisory Commission.

Denison, D. V. (2013). Debt management. In J. R. Bartle, W. B. Hildreth, & J. Marlowe (Eds.), *Management policies in local government finance* (6th ed., pp. 279–295). International City/County Management Association.

Horiuchi, C., & J. Chapman. (2019). TIF in California: Birth, growth, death and re-birth(?). In C. L. Johnson & K. Kriz (Eds.), *Tax increment financing and economic development: Uses, structures and impact* (2nd ed.). State University of New York Press

Horler, V. L. (1987). *Guide to public debt financing in California* (Rev. ed.). Packard Press.

Seufert, T. (2015). *Special financing districts*. NBS Government Finance Group.

CHAPTER 6

Economic Development

Abstract Economic development activities often have an impact on fiscal sustainability. This chapter, in its discussion of local economic development, emphasises this impact. It discusses why economic development activities should occur, identifies two key economic development strategies, and the relationship between economic development activities and debt (leading to some overlap with Chapter 5). It then identifies the governance component to economic development activities; including a discussion of three components: the approval process, the dynamic capabilities of the decision-makers, and the role of public–private partnerships. It then identifies several economic development analytic techniques but cautions that they are often ignored by economic development decision-makers. It finally identifies some initiatives that local government can use to attract economic development, and under the enabling incentive identifies two examples: special district financing and tax increment financing. It finally identifies political and equity concerns of economic development (Because the chapters can be read independently, parts of this chapter are deliberately redundant to parts of Chapter 5).

Keywords Economic development · Tax base · Job creation · Governance

J. Chapman, *The Local Budget as a Complex System*, Palgrave Studies in Public Debt, Spending, and Revenue, https://doi.org/10.1007/978-3-030-94903-7_6

Local economic development success primarily serves a two-fold purpose. It helps to ensure current fiscal sustainability and it is necessary to sustain future sustainability. This chapter will address the first issue. Chapter 7 will address the second issue.

It is almost impossible to overstate the importance of economic development to fiscal sustainability. Without economic development, the jurisdiction will become stagnant, will stop attracting new residents, and will ultimately lose its tax base. As Fig. 6.1 illustrates, economic development is an extremely complex subject and as such has an extremely complex interaction with the budget.[1] Economic development is related to local government revenues and expenditures, as well as debt decisions. It also reflects the dynamic capacity of the governance system. Before examining these interactions, there are two principal questions to consider. First, what exactly is economic development when examined from a budgetary context? The second is why should economic development be of concern to the local government—won't the free market take care of these concerns?

This study defines economic development as improvements in the tax base, the creation of jobs, or an increase in income for the citizens affected by the development. Each of these three aspects has both a revenue and expenditure impact. Increases in the tax base should increase revenues through property, sales, income, and fees and charges. As Fig. 6.1 illustrates, it does this by (hopefully) increasing both the sales and property tax bases.[2] Additionally, it is likely to increase expenditures for services provided to the developed area. From the city's perspective, the new revenues should exceed the new expenditures. Notice that these new revenues and expenditures affect both the operating and capital budgets. Depending upon the deal that the city makes with the developer, not only will there be increased service provision and tax collections but also new infrastructure provision, typically financed by new debt and additional revenues collected to finance the new debt. The budget office should be aware that the planning and economic development departments are negotiating these projects and may not be fully aware of the budgetary implications or maybe so enthused about the projects that they

[1] As in previous chapters, not every complexity issue, as indicated in Fig. 6.1, will be discussed in the text.

[2] See Fig. 3.1 for the next step in the analysis.

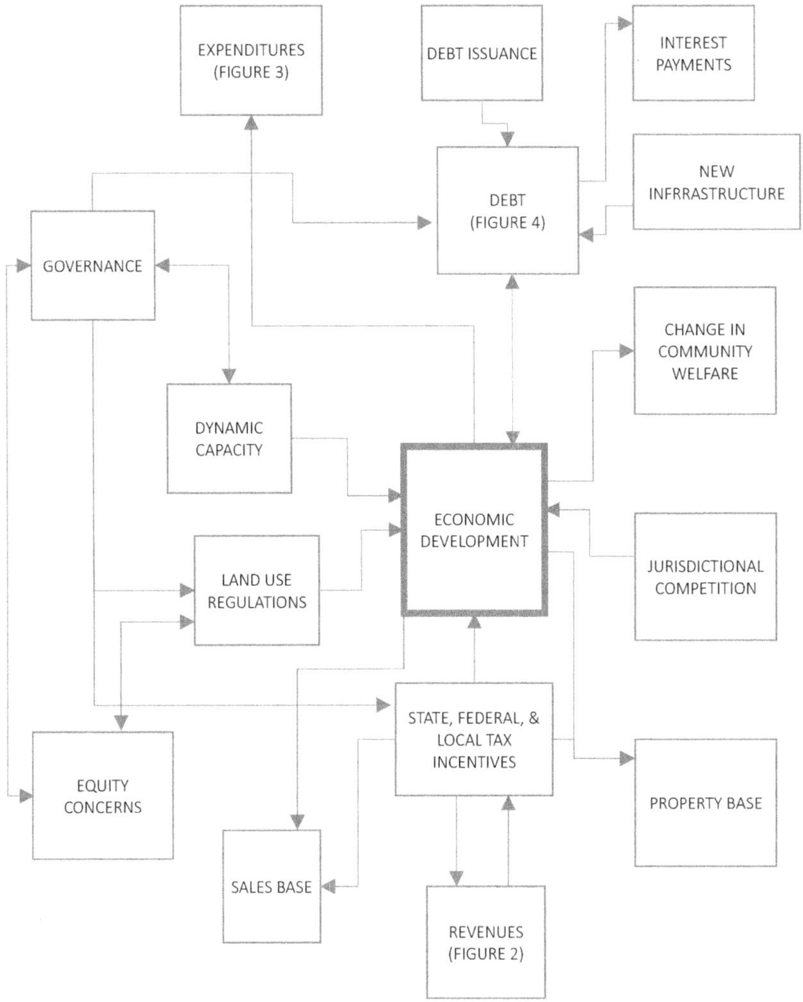

Fig. 6.1 Economic development

do not care about these implications.[3] Who does the negotiating with the developer is also a governance issue.

While a fully operating free market may be a necessary condition for a successful economic development project, it is certainly not a sufficient condition. First, significant externalities (both positive and negative) abound with any project. This means that there are likely to be uncompensated price effects that will affect the size and scope of the project. Second, there are likely to be public good attributes of the projects which if not captured by the developer might reduce its profitability and likelihood of its occurring. Third, since this development will not occur on a blank canvas, there are likely to be land use, governance, dynamic capability, and political constraints that affect its success. Further, while profits are the primary driver of the project for the developer, local governments worry about these other phenomena.

These two complexities can lead to two economic development strategies. The general approach to development attempts to create an environment that stimulates economic growth without offering targeted aid to any specific firm or industry. This means providing good infrastructure throughout the jurisdiction, lower regulatory barriers, and perhaps general tax reform. The dynamic capabilities of the jurisdiction are crucial when these requirements are being negotiated with the private sector developer. The second strategy targets the attraction of specific firms or industries, and includes tax subsidies, loans, land donations, and targeted provisions of goods and services (Mitchell et al., 2019). Although sometimes tried, the general approach is not easily available at the local level. The general approach could have a very large influence on the local budget, because it would affect all firms and industries in the city; local governments are more likely to adopt the particularistic approach and would have less of an effect on the local budget, although it would still affect both revenues and expenditures.

Before addressing some of the implications and complex interrelations among economic development concerns and the local budget, it is important to recognize that economic development influences debt, which, as Chapter 5 showed, also has an effect on the budget. This relationship has

[3] It is crucial to recognize that economic development impacts far more than the local budget. There are demographic impacts, locational impacts, sociological impacts, equity impacts, and lifestyle impacts. These may be far more important than the budgetary impacts.

to do with supplying the infrastructure for the project. Since this infrastructure will exist for a long period of time, it is a legitimate candidate for debt financing. As Fig. 6.1 hypothesizes, the more economic development activity, the greater the need for new debt. Since local governments also issue debt for non-economic development activity, there may be a future trade-off between economic development debt and debt for such things as street construction, new libraries, and new sewage systems. Further, economic development activities might tend to use more esoteric forms of debt, which will make the capital budget more difficult to understand. Since debt is closely connected with infrastructure finance, it is worthwhile to spend a brief amount of time discussing infrastructure.[4]

There seems to be a consensus that there needs to be an increase in infrastructure investment. Bennett et al. (2020) find that real infrastructure investment peaked in 1968 and then slowly declined until the early 2000s and recently has been flat, although its composition has changed; for example, investment in high tech infrastructure (broadly defined) has greatly risen since 1980. Further, the remaining useful life of state and local infrastructure also seems to be declining and depreciation profiles used to calculate the net stock of US infrastructure are more than 40 years old. Eventually, there will be more money spent on infrastructure, both new and depreciated. The question then becomes—who should pay for this infrastructure? While most economists would argue that the user should pay, if possible, they also agree that marginal cost pricing (the most efficient way of pricing) may not cover the full costs and that there are positive externalities associated with infrastructure that ought to be publicly funded. Further, there may be possibilities for using private developers' funds to help pay for the infrastructure. There is also some question as to what impact infrastructure has on economic growth rates (Glaeser & Poterba, 2020).

There is another danger. Flyvberg et al. (2004), Flyvberg (2017) claims that there is a danger of delusional optimism among planners, especially when the projects are very large. Planners tend to greatly underestimate costs for these projects. This can greatly affect the local budget, since there is a political tendency to want to finish a project once it has begun,

[4] This is closely tied to the capital improvement budget, discussed in Chapter 5.

regardless of its costs. These are long-run impacts that can affect the budget for many years in the future.[5]

An important variable in economic development is the governance orientation of the local government. There are at least three components to this.[6] The first is the approval process for the new development. As Pressman and Wildavsky (1984) demonstrated, the larger the number of steps necessary for the final approval of an economic development project, the less likelihood of project approval. Even with as high as a ninety-five percent probability of approval at each step, after only 12 clearance points within a city, the probability of successful implementation is only about fifty percent. Since it is not unusual for local government projects to have far more than 12 clearance points, there is a high likelihood of rejecting many worthwhile projects. One potential solution to this problem is a case management system, in which a city employee (usually from the planning department) shepherds the project through the approval steps. But it is not unusual if the jurisdiction ignores the implications for a sustainable budget in the rush to get the project to start.

As Fig. 6.1 shows, an additional component of governance is the dynamic capabilities of the economic development decision-makers as well as those of the mayor or city manager. These capabilities must include the ability to determine which industries are necessary to attract, based on both revenues and expenditures generated by the project, how to go about attracting those industries, and then using this evaluation to decide what are the next steps in furthering the city's economic future. This component of governance is crucial for the long-run fiscal sustainability of the jurisdiction because without appropriate economic growth, there is a risk that future public sector revenues and expenditure will not be in balance. Note that there are two dangers in the exercise of dynamic capability. The first is that the decision-makers will be too conservative. They will not be willing to push against some local complaints about the specific project (it is too high, it will increase traffic, or it will cast shade in the wrong places) or will be unwilling to take a small amount of risk that the project will not fulfill its promises. On the other hand, there may be some adventurous souls in the decision-making body who will

[5] There is likely to be an element of delusional optimism in the evaluation of specific economic incentives.

[6] There are far more than three variables. These are just examples.

be willing to undertake too much risk to attract new development. In this case, the long-run expenditures (or loss of tax revenues) will exceed the benefits of the development. It is important to clarify the long-run budgetary implications to fully utilize the dynamic capability's potential for the decision-making process.

A third variable of governance is the potential role of public–private partnerships. These can take various forms and can range from simple to complex arrangements. Salamon (2002) and Kirlin and Kirlin (1982) describe some of these arrangements. The budget office should be a participant in these discussions (as well as the legal arm of the jurisdiction). The benefits of these partnerships are that they may save the jurisdiction some money and they will emphasize the intricacies of development as seen from the private sectors views. Public–private partnerships are clearly dependent on the dynamic capabilities of the jurisdiction as well as the details of the process as it pertains to their success.[7]

Economic development planners use a variety of analytic techniques. While individuals in the budget department need not know the details of these techniques, they should be aware of their variety and use.[8] In order to employ these analytic tools, the economic development planners need to know the demographics, the local private sector economic environment, the physical and social infrastructure, and the sources of revenues and expenditures of the local budget to relate to the development. The following techniques, from Blakely and Bradshaw (2002) are dependent on this data.

Economic Base Analysis helps to decide which successful businesses, as measured by wealth generation, should be attracted and sustained. The analytic tool for this is the location quotient which examines the relationship between the local sector employment divided by total employment divided by the reference sector employment divided by the reference total employment. This quotient is useful in determining the concentration of employment and economic activity. This is a rather simplistic measure that must be carefully used when interpreting.

[7] Rodrik and Sabel (2020) argue that public–private collaboration is at the heart of building a good jobs economy, subject to this collaboration being built on good design principles.

[8] For more detail on these techniques see Blakely and Bradshaw (2002). It should be noted that in this excellent book, there is no mention of the local budget. This is another sign of why complexity analysis of the budget is useful.

Dynamic Analysis using shift-share techniques determines what types of economic activity are growing and what types are declining. Although this usually uses employment, other economic attributes are possible to use. Shift-share analysis assumes that economic growth or decline is a combination of three factors: the overall growth in the national, state, or regional economy, the relative change in an industry compared to the total of all industries, and the difference in the rate of growth (or decline) of a local industry relative to the rate of growth or decline in the same industry nationally. This measure is data intensive and used to decide if an industry has a competitive advantage in the local area. If so, it should be attracted.

Input–Output Analysis is the most sophisticated technique for examining the effects of economic changes throughout the economy. It is based on the calculated interdependencies among different economic sectors. It looks at industries from an economy-wide perspective and follows ripple effects. It models direct, indirect, and induced impacts of economic change. Local governments typically use the IMPLAN program which is a sophisticated input–output model that uses a personal computer.

Cluster Analysis is a technique used to identify regional clusters and to decide which programs to use to support the firms in the cluster. This indicates that a cluster is a set of firms that have a competitive advantage over other industries. Economic development planners use cluster analysis to develop infrastructure that supports the core firms, find gaps in supply and marketing linkages, increase the skill and training available to firms within the cluster, and help to promote clusters in the market.

In each of these techniques, and in the many others not mentioned in this monograph, there may be a "government" sector variable. But a government sector is not a budget input. Because of this, the local budget staff needs to be aware of the jurisdiction's economic development decisions, because they may have significant impacts on the fiscal sustainability of the jurisdiction. These impacts may disappear or be ignored in the morass of data collection and pages of data output that come from these techniques.

Elected officials often ignore the results of these analytic techniques when implementing economic development incentives. This is especially true when the incentives come from the national government and apply to all states and local governments. These national programs can have an impact on the local budget. For example, the Historic Tax Credits program provides a 20 percent tax credit for the rehabilitation of properties on the National Register of Historic Places. The New Markets Tax Credit program is a 39 percent federal tax credit that encourages investment in low-income census tracts. Local governments do not have full control over these federal programs. However, to the extent they are successful, they should have a positive impact on local government revenues (depending upon their treatment in terms of the local property tax). A third, more recent federal program is the Opportunity Zone program which designated thousands of areas, often using political criteria, as being economically distressed. They exist in all fifty states. There are substantial long-run tax benefits under this program. The state governors choose which areas are opportunity zones. It is too soon to comment on their effectiveness in economic development, although there is some evidence of potential favoritism in the choice of the zones by the governor (Eldar & Garber, 2019).

States also offer a variety of economic development incentives. These range from broad general incentives to incentives tied to specific industries. The intent of a typical broad-based incentive is to create jobs and increase capital investment. Some forms of these are available in almost every state. At the state level, these incentives connect to statewide tax abatements, both for property taxes and sales taxes. States also have incentives targeted to specific industries, such as agriculture, technology, manufacturing, and filmmaking. States also allow the creation of economic development zones which can allow local governments to create such activities as enterprise zones or tax increment financing (Francis, 2016). While narrower in scope than the federal incentives, state incentives are still generally broad. However, a recent Pew Foundation (2021) found that the criteria that states use to geographically target economic development are "ill-conceived or out of date" and end up serving wealthy communities instead of disadvantaged ones. Further, even when they reached the disadvantaged communities, they are often not well suited to help the residents. Still, there are effects on the local budget because they will, at least in the short run, reduce revenues (through, for example, tax abatements) in the hope that there will be long-run revenue increases.[9]

[9] See, for example, Texas Comptroller (2019).

Generally, there are two types of incentives that local governments can offer to stimulate economic development. The first are financial incentives, the second are enabling incentives. Financial incentives are typically financial aid customized to either individual businesses or industries. The intent of these incentives is to encourage business growth (Bartik, 2020) as well as increase jobs and incomes.[10] Some examples of these incentives are tax credits which can reduce a tax liability, such as property tax credits (local budgetary effects) or corporate taxes (state budgetary effects). In some cases, these tax credits are refundable. So even if the firm has no tax liability, it still receives these credits. Examples of these incentives are job creation credits or grants, property tax abatements, and research and development credits (Bartik, 2020). These direct financial incentives cost state and local governments about $46 billion (Bartik, 2020). Justification for these incentives comes from using a "but for" argument. That is, it is argued, the firm or industry would not locate in the particular jurisdiction "but for" these incentives. In practice, these financial incentives are controversial. They tend to go to big businesses rather than small, incentive expenditures are increasing (perhaps indicating incentive wars), and the incentives probably do not make much difference in firm location—that is the "but for" argument is specious. For example, Bartik (2018) found that the typical incentive probably tips somewhere between 2 and 25 percent of the favored firms to locate in the incentive providing jurisdiction. There may be cases in which the dynamic capacity attributes of the local decision-makers cause more problems than necessary. Finally, only 30 states have regularized procedures to decide whether these fiscal incentives meet their promised goals. Many of these states have begun to mandate clawback provisions, in which the incentivized firm must repay the incentive if the firm doesn't meet its promises.

Most states enable local governments to form special financing districts (sometimes called benefit-assessment districts) to provide needed services (Seufert, 2015). These districts can be varied, including lighting districts, park districts, and business improvement districts. They can collect revenues from residents within the district to provide needed infrastructure and services. This mechanism takes revenue and expenditures for a particular sub-section of the jurisdiction out of the local budget and

[10] It is rare that their effects on tax revenues that can be generated from this growth are prominently mentioned in the academic literature.

makes the residents of the jurisdiction responsible for paying for the benefits that the district provides. One of the most important kinds of these districts is the community facilities district. Depending upon the state law, developers can form these districts when building a new subdivision under the authority of the city, county, or school district. They collect non-ad valorem property taxes to fund a variety of services, including police, fire, recreation programs, park maintenance, and flood and storm protection as well as several types of capital infrastructure. These can generate large budget savings for the jurisdiction if it is expanding. However, they are very difficult to implement for developed areas.[11]

A particular theoretical method of financing development (both new and redevelopment) is to use the increase in land value that occurs because of the development as a basis for collecting revenues. Although seldom used in its pure form in the United States, this value capture technique is sometimes used in other countries (Chapman, 2015). It forms the theoretical basis for the implementation of tax increment financing (TIF), a technique used in 48 states.[12] Using this procedure, local governments fund economic development activities in a designated area within the jurisdiction by earmarking the property tax increment that occurs because of redevelopment activity. The non-increment continues to flow to the governments that were using these revenues prior to the establishment of the Tax Increment District. Because there is often infrastructure constructed, bonds are often issued with the increment supporting this issuance. In many states, a finding of blight must occur before the establishment of the district. The district, in most states, is established by action of the city council, without voter approval. The argument for this method is the "but for" argument—without the district, development would not occur. A redevelopment agency, not the city council, administers the tax increment district.[13] This is the agency that issues the debt (without a public vote for approval) and works with the private developer to redevelop the property. While this can be a very useful tool, it also has the potential for misuse—how is blight determined, what is the correct size of the district, is the "but for" argument valid, and how is the potential

[11] See Chapter 4 for more information on these districts.

[12] California eliminated Tax Increment Financing in 2012 and has since replaced it with Enhanced Infrastructure Financing Districts (Day, 2016). Arizona does not have this law. Also see Chapter 5 for a discussion of TIF.

[13] Although in many cases, the redevelopment agency is made up of the city council.

lost revenue to other agencies replaced (Merriman, 2018). This technique can be a double-edged sword for the local budget. If the area was truly blighted and the "but for" explanation is valid, the budgetary effects are minimal (assuming the increment also covers any potential increased service demands). However, if there is no blight in the area, the overlapping local governments which would gain property tax revenues from the district are penalized, since at least some of the new property tax increment really belongs to them, not the redevelopment agency. This may particularly impact school districts. This reason is why California abandoned TIF—the state had to backfill lost school district revenues, and this backfill became huge (Horiuchi & Chapman, 2019; Lefcoe & Swenson, 2014).

There are at least three political struggles associated with these economic development incentives. Again, while they may seem tangential to the city budget process, their long-run implications can be fiscally harmful, and the budget should anticipate their occurrence. The first struggle can be between specific areas in the jurisdiction. This struggle involves which area needs economic development the most, which is the easiest to implement development practices, and which has the political power. Demonstrations of these struggles occur in the choice of the location of tax increment financing areas or in the location of Opportunity Zones. It may also be that some areas need redevelopment, but they do not want to have development occur near them (the Not in my Back Yard syndrome). This struggle may also include environmental justice concerns.

The second political struggle elates to competition among states (or within states, among cities) for the location and development of firms and industries. This competition often involves subsidies, tax abatements, discounted land prices, and infrastructure provision (Rolnick & Burstein, 1995). Clever firms and industries can generate a race to the bottom effect, where the incentives are so large that some public services may have to have their budgets reduced in order to finance the incentive. The local government budget office must stay on top of these negotiations because of their budget ramifications.

The third political struggle occurs when there are overlapping jurisdictions that share the same tax base but who have unequal political power (or unequal dynamic capacity). For example, a school district's property tax base can overlap both the county and city base. If the city allows a tax increment district to form, the school districts may lose potential property tax revenue.[14] In this case, the increment goes solely to the redevelopment agency.

It may also be that those specific incentives tailored to specific firms or industries are often a second level of importance to the firm's relocation decisions. They often do not work and further, when they do work, the benefits of the firm's relocation do not exceed the costs. Often, local economic development decision-makers ignore the fiscal sustainability implications of these incentives to the determinant of the jurisdiction. It is far better for the jurisdiction to try to improve the general environment for business attraction. Thus, zoning and land use restrictions, overall tax rates, transportation availability, an educated workforce, and good schools are far more likely to be important than a specific subsidy. It appears that only in rare cases would a direct subsidy tip the balance for a firm's decision.

There are two other sets of variables that impact economic development activities. Although discussed separately, they are closely connected with both mitigating and worsening effects based on their connectivity. The first is the extent of the jurisdiction's concern about equity in economic development. Figure 6.1 hypothesizes that governance, land use regulations, and equity concerns, through the impact of land use regulations that affect economic development. There is some evidence that some economic development projects—particularly those projects that have negative externalities but are necessary for overall economic development such as airports or sewage treatment plants—may be located near population areas that have little political power. These tend to have minority and low-income populations. The environmental justice movement raises these issues as examples of non-equitable economic development (Campbell et al., 2015). These location decisions may further lead to lawsuits which will prevent, at least for a time, the completion of the projects. Closely related to the environmental justice concern is a broad concern about equity. It is necessary to explicitly consider who are the beneficiaries of the economic development projects and who may be the losers. For example, are opportunity zones supplying jobs for the low and moderate workers or are they attracting workers from

[14] This scenario is partially responsible for California ending tax increment financing. The state was responsible for backfilling school district lost revenue because of tax increment financing. Over time, this backfilling became extremely expensive, so the state got out of this predicament by stopping the program.

other parts of the jurisdiction and thus exacerbating income distribution problems (Wessel, 2021). Additionally, property values may rise in the developing areas which could translate into rent increases which will affect poor people who were living in lower rent apartments. Finally, if the development involves retail sales, some store owners outside of the redevelopment project area might see their sales fall while the sales in the new area increase.

The second variable is the extent of growth management. While zoning is important to ensure certainty in developing (no one wants to buy a house if it is unknown if a sewage plant will be located next door), it can also restrict development. While the economics might argue in favor of a high-rise development, zoning restrictions endorsed by the neighborhood might only allow low rise construction. This could force sales tax generating activities to locate outside of the jurisdiction. There is also some evidence that residential zoning restrictions have led to a housing shortage and therefore an increase in housing prices, again having equity implications (Ellickson, 2020). Different jurisdictions may address equity concerns in different ways. While some may ignore them in the short run, this is not a long-run fiscal sustainability way of addressing these issues. Well-managed cities should have these concerns always acknowledged. The budget function in the jurisdiction has a vital role to play in ensuring that the jurisdiction includes equity concerns in the analysis. They should also be part of the forecasting of long-run revenues and expenditures, especially when incorporating the fiscal effects of the economic development project into the city budget.

Despite—or perhaps because of—its importance, there are often political barriers to economic development projects. Using the equity concerns as noted above, neighborhood action groups may try to stop projects. Or, using their self-interest as a motivation, other neighborhood action groups might also attempt to stop projects. While lack of political support and citizen opposition are not the principal barriers to economic development (cost and availability of land are the two principal barriers), they are not unimportant (Reese & Sands, 2013). These political barriers may be wise if the project doesn't help to lead to fiscal sustainability; they may not be wise if the project does not contribute to fiscal sustainability. Not in my backyard (NIMBY) motivations can thus be either good or bad, but they should always lead to careful analysis at the city level—which includes a careful fiscal sustainability analysis. To the extent that there is good governance in the local community and the decision-makers demonstrate a high level of dynamic capacity, a jurisdiction can overcome these political barriers to good development.[15]

To conclude, the Government Finance Officers Association (2018) emphasizes that an economic development policy should explicitly have the following elements: identify the goals and objectives of economic development, define the application and limitations of the chosen incentive tools, and have a clearly defined evaluation process. Note that the effects of economic development on the budget are subsumed within these categories. This monograph argues that understanding economic development policy is a necessary part of a complex understanding of fiscal sustainability budgeting and GFOA should also emphasize their importance.

Bibliography

Bartik, T. J. (2018). *"But for" percentages of economic development incentives: What percentage estimates are plausible based on the research literature?* (Upjohn Institute Working Paper 18–289). Upjohn Institute.

Bartik, T. J. (2020, May). Introduction to special issue: Learning more about incentives. *Economic Development Quarterly, 34*(2), 1–6.

Bennett, J., Kornfeld, R., Sichel, D., & Wasshausen, D. (2020, December). *Measuring infrastructure in the bureau of economic analysis national income accounts* (BEA Working Paper Series, W2020-12). Retrieved May 5, 2021.

Blakely, E. J., & Bradshaw, T. K. (2002). *Planning local economic development* (3rd ed.). Sage Publications.

Campbell, H. E., Eckerd, A. M., & Kim, Y. (2015). *Rethinking environmental justice in sustainable cities: Insights from agent based modeling*. Routledge.

Chapman, J. I. (2015). *Annotated bibliography on land value taxation and value capture*. Lincoln Institute of Land Policy.

Day, L. (2016, August 31). *A new financing tool for California: Enhanced infrastructure finance districts*. Retrieved June 1, 2021, from www.Planetizen.com/node/88347/new-financing-tool-california-enhanced-infrastructure-finance-districts

[15] Institutional effects on economic development have long been studied at the national level (e.g., Putnam, 1993). Recently, there has been some interest in examining local government institutions apart from governance issues as they effect economic development (Gomez et al., 2016). However, for the purpose of this monograph, governance and institutions will be in the same typology.

Eldar, O., & Garber, C. (2019, October 3). *Does government play favorites? Evidence from opportunity zones*. Retrieved October 31, 2019, from https://ssrn.com/abstract=3463541

Ellickson, R. C. (2020, January 13). *Zoning and the cost of housing: Evidence from Silicon Valley, greater New Haven, and greater Austin*. Retrieved June 2, 2021, from https://ssrn.com/abstract=3472145 or https://doi.org/10.2139/ssrn.3472145

Flyvberg, B. (2017). Introduction: The iron law of megaproject management. In B. Flyvberg (Ed.), *The Oxford handbook of megaproject management* (Chapter 1, pp. 1–18). Oxford University Press. Retrieved May 22, 2020, from https://www.researchgate.net/publication/299393235_Introduction_The_Iron_Law_of_Megaproject_Management

Flyvberg, B., Glenting, C., & Ronnest, A. (2004, June). *Procedures for dealing with optimism bias in transport planning*. British Department for Transport. The British department for transport, guidance document. Retrieved May 22, 2020, from https://papers.ssrn.com/sol3/papers.cfm?abstract_id=2278346

Francis, N. (2016, February 29). State tax incentives for economic development. *Urban Institute Brief*. Urban Institute, Washington D.C. https://www.urban.org/research/publication/state-tax-incentives-economic-development. Accessed 28 May 2021.

Glaeser, E. L., & Poterba, J. M. (2020, December). *Economic analysis and infrastructure investment* (NBER Working Paper Series, Working Paper 28215). Retrieved May 22, 2020, from http://www.nber.org/papers/w28215

Gomez, G., Knorringa, P., & Gomez, G. M. (2016). *Local governance, economic development and institutions*. Macmillan.

Government Finance Officers Association. (2018). *Best practice: Economic development incentive policies*. Government Finance Officers Association. Retrieved September 29.

Horiuchi, C., & Chapman, J. (2019). TIF in California: Birth, growth, death and re-birth(?). In C. L. Johnson & K. Kriz (Eds.), *Tax increment financing and economic development: Uses, structures and impact* (2nd ed., Chapter 9). State University of New York Press

Kirlin, J. J., & Kirlin, A. M. (1982). *Public choices—Private resources*. California Tax Foundation.

Lefcoe, G., & C. W. Swenson. (2014, August). Redevelopment in California: The demise of TIF-funded redevelopment in California and its aftermath. *National Tax Journal, 67*(September), 719–744.

Merriman, D. (2018). *Improving tax increment financing (TIF) for economic development*. Lincoln Institute of Land Policy, Policy focus Report. Retrieved May 31, 2021, from https://www.lincolninstitute.edu/publications/policy-focus-reports/improving-tax-increment-financing-tif-economic-development

Mitchell, M. D., Farren, M. D., Horpedahl, J., & Gonzalez, O. (2019, November). *The economics of a targeted economic development subsidy*. Mercatus Special Study. Mercatus Center, George Mason University. Retrieved May 5, 2020.

Pew Charitable Trusts. (2021, February). *How states can direct economic development to places and people in need*. Pewtrusts.org. Retrieved May 30, 2021, from https://www.pewtrusts.org/en/research-and-analysis/reports/2021/02/how-states-can-direct-economic-development-to-places-and-people-in-need

Pressman, J., & Wildavsky, A. (1984). *Implementation*. University of California Press.

Putnam, R. (1993). *Making democracy work: Civic traditions in modern Italy*. Princeton University Press.

Reese, L. A., & Sands, G. (2013). Local economic development. In J. R. Bartle, W. B. Hildreth, & J. Marlowe (Eds.), *Management Policies in Local Government Finance* (6th ed., pp. 319–344). International City/County Management Association.

Rodrik, D., & Sabel, C. (2020, January). *Building a good jobs economy* (Harvard Kennedy School Faculty Research Working Paper, RWP20-001). Retrieved May 20, 2020.

Rolnick, A. J., & Burstein, M. L. (1995, January 1). *Congress should end the economic war among the states*. Federal Reserve Bank of Minneapolis. Retrieved June 1, 2021, from https://www.minneapolisfed.org/article/1995/congress-should-end-the-economic-war-among-the-states

Salamon, L. M. (2002). *The tools of government*. Oxford University Press.

Seufert, T. (2015). *Special financing districts*. NBS Government Finance Group.

Texas Comptroller of Public Accounts. (2019, June). *Tax-related state and Local economic development programs*. Retrieved May 30, 2021, from https://gov.texas.gov/business/page/incentives

Wessel, D. (2021). *Only the rich can play*. Public Affairs.

CHAPTER 7

The Interrelationships of Dynamic Complexity in Budgeting

Abstract This chapter integrates complexity theory, dynamic capabilities, and the budget in the overall governance framework of the facilitative state. The facilitative state not only is responsible for service provision but also as an active participant in determining service expenditures and revenues. In this section, the goal of the facilitative state is to increase the welfare level of its inhabitants. The chapter then gives examples of this logic of the complex system involving interactions between revenue's and expenditure's economic development and expenditures, and dynamic capabilities and debt. The chapter finally identifies three outcomes of this complex system: bankruptcy, static budget sustainability, and improvements in the welfare of the residents of the jurisdiction.

Keywords Facilitative state · Complexity · Dynamic capabilities bankruptcy

The goal of this chapter is to show how to use complexity theory to understand the dynamics of local budgeting. It puts the previously discussed variables into a complex model reflecting these dynamics. These dynamics can lead to three potential outcomes: a lack of fiscal sustainability, or bankruptcy; stability of fiscal sustainability at the current level

J. Chapman, *The Local Budget as a Complex System*, Palgrave Studies in Public Debt, Spending, and Revenue, https://doi.org/10.1007/978-3-030-94903-7_7

of budgeting; or, fiscal sustainability at a higher level of welfare for the residents of the jurisdiction. To do this, the chapter uses the concept of the facilitative state and its impacts on both governance and dynamic capabilities. Both fiscal sustainability and budgeting are dynamic concepts. This chapter describes the framework used to understand these dynamic components. The most important part of this framework is Newland's concept of the facilitative state, as augmented to include the budgeting process. While Newland (1984) focused on the national government and defined the facilitation of effective constitutional democracy as the public purpose, conceptually, his reasoning can be applied at the local level—government is not only expected to ensure that its traditional activities are occurring but it is also expected to facilitate the activities of a myriad of actors as they also attempt to accomplish the purposes of local government as financed through the budget process (see Newland, 1998, 2003, 2007, 2008 for significant extensions). This definition envisions the state as not merely a provider of services but also as an active participant in the determination of service financing, mix, and level. It is in this sense that the state participates in governance activities as well as encouraging dynamic capacity. The role of the local government, in this case, does not necessarily lead to conclusions about the size of the local government. The definition is consistent with both a jurisdiction that has a small budget as well as a jurisdiction that has a large budget. The facilitative state allows the governance function to respond to a changing world in a multiple set of dimensions as opposed to a focus on the one best way of accomplishing its goals. Thus, the definition of the facilitative state at the local level is that it is an institutional framework that allows local government to use a variety of governance activities to increase the welfare of its residents. Defining the facilitative state in this manner explicitly argues that the goals of local government are to increase the welfare of its residents, allow a variety of governance techniques to exist, and to encourage dynamic complexity. Further, it is an institutional mechanism that allows and encourages change over time—a necessary concern for maintaining fiscal sustainability. In this sense, the definition allows responses to both exogenous changes that affect the local government (think pandemic or housing bubbles) as well as endogenous changes (think special districts as not generating enough revenue to cover expenditures). As a by-product, conceptualizing the local government as a facilitator, encourages good governance practices because it allows for competing notions of how to accomplish government's tasks.

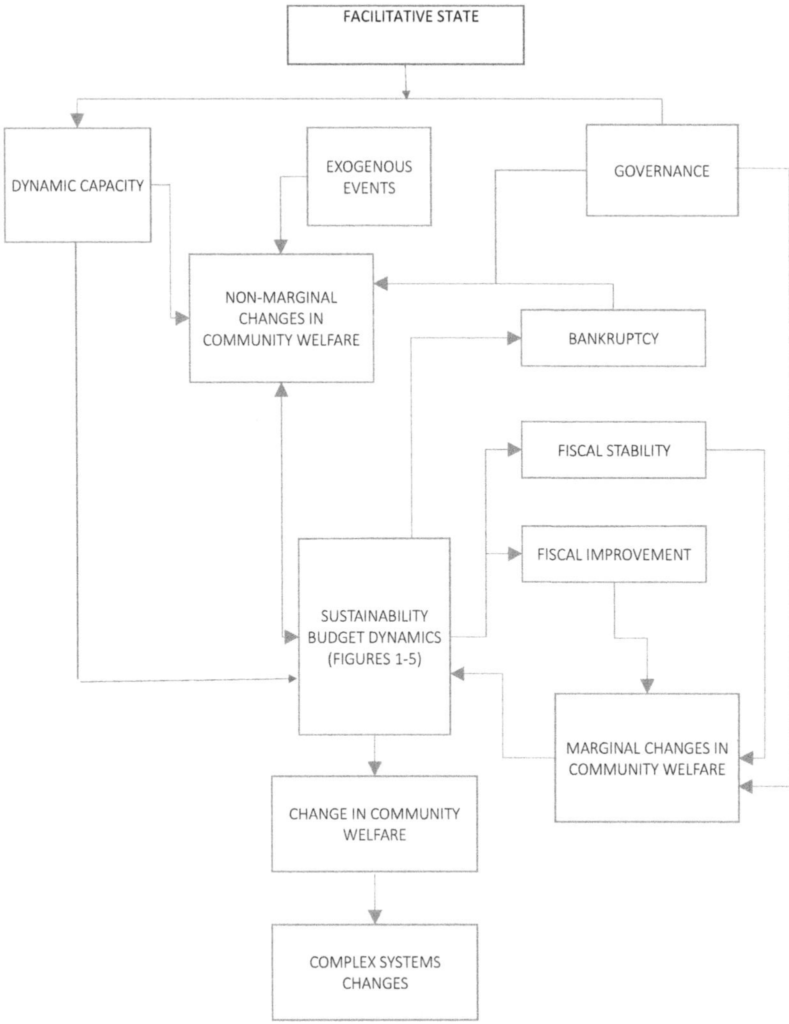

Fig. 7.1 Dynamic complexity theory and the budget

Figure 7.1 highlights the importance of the facilitative state. Its existence has an impact on both governance issues and dynamic capacity capabilities. Because the facilitative state allows flexibility in governance activities, it potentially allows the governance decision-makers to address the complexity of the budget process in a variety of manners. They may use different budget formats, different budget techniques, and different budget decision rules, all of which appear in most budgeting textbooks. Because the complexity of the system, as illustrated in Figs. 1.1, 3.1, 4.1, 5.1, and 6.1, makes it difficult to forecast accurately long-run fiscal sustainability, the governance system must have the flexibility to respond to both endogenous and exogenous events. While, for example, tax and expenditure limitations, which are exogenous to the system, constrain this flexibility, the ability and complexity of the system allows for some work-arounds to maintain sustainability. While some of these alternative techniques to deal with constraints may be clear to the decision-makers, others may not be transparent and may lead to a worsening of the fiscal situation. For example, how many city council members really understand the use of Certificates of Participation to avoid General Obligation debt limits.[1] The complexity of the entire system also increases the likelihood of endogenous changes. A change in one element of the tax increment financing process can affect economic development fiscal forecasts, debt issuance ability, and ultimately both revenue and expenditure and debt elements of fiscal sustainability. The decisions that come from governance decisions in addressing both these exogenous and endogenous changes will influence the next cycle of fiscal sustainability analysis.

The facilitative state also affects the dynamic capabilities of the jurisdiction, which in turn may affect its governance ability. Fiscally sustainable local governments may well attract both innovative residents and innovative public sector managers. Just as the Tiebout model (1956) argues that residents choose jurisdictions that meet their tastes and preferences for services and taxes, it is reasonable to assume that a taste for fiscally successful government is also part of these tastes and preferences. This would be especially true in the governance function. With high capability in the governance function, there should be a greater ability to address successfully both marginal and non-marginal changes that occur because of exogenous and endogenous events. Although not explicitly addressed in this monograph, there may be a feedback loop between good governance and high dynamic capability. Of course, this loop can be bad as

[1] A Certificate of Participation is a type of debt that is structured as a lease and is not classified as debt for purposes of debt limits and voter approval. It is very arcane.

well as good—low dynamic capability can lead to poor governance decisions which can feedback into a continuing decline in dynamic capability (as well as a concurrent decline in population). Jurisdictions with high dynamic capacity may be both reactive to outside and inside changes or proactive, finding that they must identify changes and then attempt to make those changes. With high governance and dynamic capacity, the jurisdiction should be not only in a situation of fiscal sustainability but also in one of maximizing the community's welfare. This situation would provide the background for increasing growth over time with constant positive feedback. But with poor governance and dynamic capability, the jurisdiction could end up in a continuing fiscal crisis.

To avoid this crisis, it is crucial that the budgeting system understands the interactions among all the components of the model and address the budget as an outcome of a complex system. This next section of this chapter will give some partial examples of the complexity of the interactions. Most of these complex interactions initially occur in the sustainability budget dynamics cell of Fig. 7.1 and then spill over into several different outcomes.

Revenues and Expenditures: In most of the public finance literature, beginning with Bergstrom and Goodman (1973), it is hypothesized that the amount of local public expenditures depends upon their tax price, with a higher tax price associated with a lower level of public spending. In terms of the fiscal sustainability equation, this implies that as the present value of revenues increases, the present value of expenditures decreases. However, it is not unusual for the local government to face demand to provide some services, regardless of the potential revenue shortfall. In these cases, the local government must increase taxes or fees to ensure the financing of the necessary level of service. In this case, revenues are a function of expenditures, with higher expenditures associated with higher revenues. Furthermore, if economic development expenditures increase, it could well lead to an increase in revenues in the next budget year. If the present value of the future revenue increases is larger than the current expenditure increases, then there is a maintenance of fiscal sustainability. This is a case in which an increase in expenditures will lead to an increase in revenues. Since the local planners may not be concerned with how to finance their projects, the staff responsible for the budget function of the jurisdiction may find themselves in some serious negotiations with other departments. Or suppose revenues increase for some exogenous reason. It may be that instead of cutting taxes to keep the same level of revenues, the city may decide to expand services. This is the case in which an increase in revenues leads to an increase in services. This relationship will be quite important to the local budget, because unless there is the certainty that the new revenue level will continue, there may be future deficits necessary to cover the new expenditures.

Economic development and service expenditures: Most jurisdictions think of economic development projects as a way of increasing the number of jobs in the city, the value of land in the city, or an increase in personal income for at least some residents of the city.[2] The budgetary revenue benefits of these measures are often casually calculated and are frequently assumed to offset the city expenditures, even after the decrease in taxes collected that occurs because of various development tax incentives. However, the delineation of the new city expenditures necessary to support this new development may not regularly occur. However, a successful new development will require expansion of city services—more police, more sewage treatment, more water supply, and maybe more parks and recreation and libraries, depending upon the project. The budget function must make careful calculations as to these new costs and compare them to the new, estimated, revenues generated by the development. Additionally, it is likely that debt finance for the capital infrastructure is necessary, which requires a debt service analysis. Depending upon the type of debt issued, and the pattern of debt repayment, there are both fixed and variable costs. If the jurisdiction does not use some sort of value capture technique, then the debt will have to be financed from other sources, including potentially the General Fund. In this case, the budget function and the treasury functions become closely connected.

Dynamic capability and debt: Figure 7.1 illustrates that while governance capacity influences sustainability budget dynamics through its effects on marginal changes in community welfare, it hypothesizes that dynamic capacity can directly influence these budget dynamics. There are many ways that a jurisdiction can respond to significant revenue constraints or increased demand for expenditures: it can cut services, it can attempt to raise taxes, or it can develop new innovative ways of financing its business. The success of the innovation response reflects

[2] The city must be cautious in calculating the value of these benefits. For example, the new jobs might be given to people in the city who do not live around the redevelopment area so these benefits may be inequitable distributed.

the dynamic capability of the jurisdiction. One instance of the innovative responses involves municipal debt. For example, to finance the public infrastructure for new development, especially when there are tax limits, the state legislatures invented the concept of community facilities districts that local governments can use. As earlier shown, these districts can issue debt financed by new taxes (generally non-ad valorem property taxes). A second example might be the Enhanced Infrastructure Financing Districts that replaced tax increment financing in California (Amador, 2016). Less than a decade old, this entirely new form of governance allows the financing of new infrastructure using a variant of value capture tax theory combined with intergovernmental coordination and a public vote. Both examples indicate a role for the local government budget department because they both have fiscal sustainability implications.

It is also necessary to discuss the timing of the components of fiscal sustainability. The implicit assumption is that decisions, impacts, and responses occur instantaneously. While it is beyond the scope of this monograph to fully explore the implications of relaxing this assumption, it is possible to give some indications of the implications of adding a time dimension to the interactions. For example, fiscal sustainability is both a short-run and a long-run concept. In the short run, the jurisdiction might cover a deficit by using the dynamic capabilities of the budget department or city council. That is, while legally required to have a balanced budget, there are clever ways of covering a short-term deficit. Eventually, however, there are consequences of not meeting the constraints of fiscal sustainability.[3]

Short-run impacts may have long-term consequences. For example, suppose there is an unexpected exogenous change in the short run, perhaps an unanticipated mandate that affects the budget (see Fig. 7.1).[4] Responses to this change may solve short-run problems but exacerbate long-term potential problems. Perhaps it is necessary to exploit the dynamic capacity of the governance system to solve the short-run problem and new types of debt are issued or the jurisdiction institutes unique economic development projects. These can have long-run feedback effects on other components of the system, which in turn can change

[3] In application, since next year's budget is usually only a marginal change from the current budget, long-run sustainability should be achievable.

[4] Community welfare is a phrase that represents the aggregate well being of the residents of the jurisdiction.

the fiscal sustainability results. Eventually, there may be changes in the revenue and expenditure characteristics of the jurisdiction which under the Tiebout model would influence the demography of the jurisdiction. The changes in population would then affect the potential success of the economic development projects and, if the electorate changes, may affect the governance system.[5]

There are at least three outcomes in this complex system. Each of these represents distinct responses to the large number of variables in this complex system. The first outcome is bankruptcy, which can occur either slowly or quickly.[6] Slow bankruptcy occurs when there is no achievement of fiscal sustainability in any one year but there are ad hoc budget adjustments that hide the problem. These short-run solutions, which really are not stable solutions, feedback into the complex system and ultimately exacerbate the fiscal situation. To avoid long-term bankruptcy in this situation may involve making non-marginal choices in the expenditures, revenue, or retirement benefits. Quick bankruptcy occurs when the governance system realizes that the fiscal situation is hopeless if all the slow bankruptcy trends continue, and the only solution is to declare bankruptcy rather than stretch out the process.

A second outcome is budget stability. The budget is sustainable and adjusted for inflation and the components of sustainability do not change.[7] There will be no decline in services, although there will be no increase in services. There will be no addressing of any existing equity problems. Real revenue changes will correspond to real expenditure changes. There will be no real economic changes in the budget. While stability may seem to be boring, it does provide the jurisdiction time to plan for its future. However, long-run stability will prove to be a challenge. As seen, there are too many variables that influence the budget and if any of them change, as this complex system has shown, stability is not likely to exist. In this case, there is no guarantee that the jurisdiction will be at its optimum welfare level—only that it is meeting the fiscal

[5] Another, more prosaic example is changing the pension system (or OPEBs system) in order to attract more city workers.

[6] Local government bankruptcy almost never happens. However, what often saves cities from going bankrupt is exogenous state or federal aid. In this monograph, in a diversion from reality, bankruptcy is defined as realizing that fiscal sustainability can never be reached and so the jurisdiction shrinks away to nothing.

[7] All appropriately discounted.

sustainability requirements. In this case, there may be citizen demands for changes in revenue or expenditure patterns that both maintain sustainability and increase resident welfare. This is the situation in many cities where there are political conflicts as to the future path of the city.

The third outcome is improvement in the welfare of the residents of the jurisdiction which comes from fiscal sustainability at a higher citizen welfare level. In this situation, depending upon the tastes and preferences of the residents of the jurisdiction, fiscal sustainability will be at the highest welfare level for the community. This may be at a high level of revenues, expenditures, and other components of fiscal sustainability or at a low level. But in either case, it will be at an optimum.

The Appendix gives a graphical interpretation of these outcomes.

There are two basic conclusions from this complex system analysis. The first is that the budget is a part of a very complex system with many interactions. The second is that dynamic capacity and the governance system are closely related, and this relationship must be taken advantage of in order to solve budget problems.

Figures 1.1 through 7.1 are a simplified demonstration of the complexity of the budget makers world. While this monograph did not discuss all the components, there are a great many interactions among them in each figure. This implies that each component may have at least two impacts on fiscal sustainability. The first is the direct impact, the second is an indirect impact that comes from the interaction. These complex interactions within each figure then must be taken into account by the analysis of the other figures. A particular concept in Fig. 1.1 is likely to have an impact on a concept in Fig. 6.1 and together (as Fig. 7.1 indicates) they affect the budget and the ability of the jurisdiction to be fiscally sustainable and ultimately jurisdictional welfare. This implies that the people who put the budget together must treat the process as a system. They cannot work in a siloed atmosphere. If they are not aware of the interactions, a great deal can go wrong as the budget unfolds.

There will always be unforeseen budget problems for any jurisdiction. To address these problems, the jurisdiction must consciously encourage its staff to develop a dynamic capacity. They must create a culture of careful entrepreneurial advancement so that when the budget problems unexpectedly arise, the managers are able to develop solutions that not only take into account the systemic complexity of the budget process but are also innovative and doable. This means that they must embrace the model of the facilitative state to incorporate both the complexity of the budget as well as the dynamic capabilities of the governance system. For example, they may want to undertake projects that involve citizen participation in the provision of services, or they may want to engage the private sector in a variety of ways in the provision of services. They should learn to use the complexity and interactions within the system as assets rather than liabilities. While this may make the job of producing a fiscally sustainable budget more difficult, eventually there will be great benefits to accepting these new requirements.

Bibliography

Amador, C. (2016). *Enhanced infrastructure financing districts*. California Community Economic Development Association.

Bergstrom, T. C., & Goodman, R. P. (1973, June). Private demands for public goods. *The American Economic Review, 63*(3), 280–296.

Newland, C. A. (1984). *Public administration and community: Realism in the practice of ideals*. Public Administration Service.

Newland, C. A. (1998). Competitiveness and the public service, the facilitative state. *Korea and the global community: Korea 50 years* (Constitutional Celebration) (pp. 83–96). Korean Institute of Public Administration.

Newland, C. A. (2003, September). The facilitative state, political executive aggrandizement and public service challenges. *Administration and Society, 35*(4), 379–407.

Newland, C. A. (2007). Accountability for responsible American governance in today's facilitative state/garrison state era. In D. Argyriades, O. P. Dwivedi, & J. G. Jabbra (Eds.), *Public administration in transition* (pp. 24–46). Vallentine Mitchell.

Newland, C. A. (2008). Public administration amid turbulence: Facilitation of enhanced future governance? *International Journal of Organization Theory and Behavior, 11*(3), 326–354.

Tiebout, C. M. (1956). A pure theory of local expenditures. *Journal of Political Economy, 64*(5), 416–424.

Appendix

While all cities want to be in a position of having a fiscally sustainable pattern of revenuesand expenditures, it is not true that all cities want that sustainability to be at the same revenue and expenditure level. Some cities may want to have a very large public sector, in terms of both revenues and expenditures; other cities may prefer to have a smaller public sector. A simplified explanation follows.

Figure A.1a illustrates what a balanced budget would look like. The 45-degree line shows the situation in which the present value of the revenues (see Fig. 3.1) equals the present value of all expenditures (see Fig. 4.1). This represents fiscal sustainability. If the budget is to the left of this line, it is running a surplus (perhaps banking it in a rainy-day fund). To the right of the line, it is running a deficit, which eventually is unsustainable. The question becomes, where on the line is a particular jurisdiction.

Assuming Tieboutmobility, it means that the residents of the jurisdiction have similar tastes and preferences concerning the relative sizes of the public and private sectors. In this case, a social welfare function can be determined, representing trade-offs between the public and private sectors. With similar tastes and preferences (if not identical), this function would be the sum of the utility functions of the inhabitants. With Tiebout sorting, different jurisdictions would have different social

J. Chapman, *The Local Budget as a Complex System*, Palgrave Studies in Public Debt, Spending, and Revenue, https://doi.org/10.1007/978-3-030-94903-7

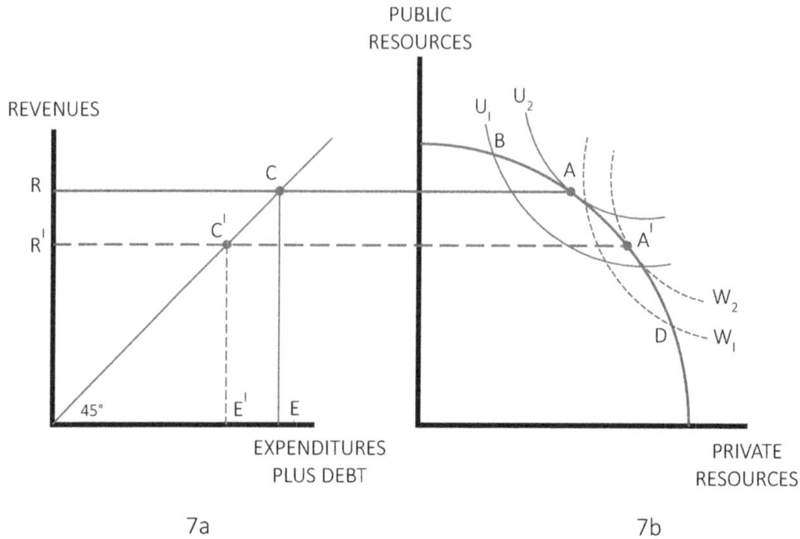

Fig. A.1 Tiebout mobility and the budget

welfare functions. Figure A.1b shows two different social welfare functions representing two different jurisdictions. The map of these social welfare functions is interpreted in the same manner as that of simple consumer utility theory—the farther away from the origin, the greater the social welfare.

The production possibility frontier in this model illustrates the trade-off between the size of the public sector (as measured by the budget) and the size of the private sector. It follows the traditional assumption of being concave to the origin, showing diminishing marginal returns. In the short run, it assumes an existing technology for the private sector and an existing governance system and dynamic capacity for the public sector. As these variables increase, the production possibility frontier moves out.

The tangency of the community social welfare function and the production possibilities frontier shows the maximum welfare for the particular community, given its production possibilities frontier.[1] If for some reason the community with social welfare functions U_1 and U_2

[1] While not exactly Bator's (1957) "bliss point" it is somewhat analogous.

finds itself at point B, it can improve its welfare by reducing its consumption (i.e., the budget) of the public sector and increasing its consumption of private goods, thereby moving from point B to point A and therefore moving to a higher social welfare function. Note that the second community with the different social welfare functions, W_1 and W_2, point A' is the optimum, which has a different allocation of resources than the first community. This illustrates it is feasible for different communities to have different tastes and preferences and thus demand different bundles of public and private goods.

There is a connection between Fig. A.1a, b. Once point A is determined, it then can be traced to the 45-degree line in Fig. A.1a. This gives the fiscally sustainable level of revenuesand expenditures that is associated with point A, that is point C. There is also a point C' that is the fiscal equivalent for the second jurisdiction.

The governance system is the mechanism that moves the community point B to point A in Fig. A.1b. In this example, there is too large a public sector at B, so using the tools of governance, there should be a budget reduction—it is still fiscally sustainable but at a lower level. For example, off-loading some of governmental expenditures onto the private sector through public–private partnerships or developing new service-providing mechanisms such as community facilities districts would lower the municipal budget. Conversely, if the second community is at point D, it indicates a greater level of taxes and expenditures. This could involve going to the voters for approval of new taxes,(justified by being attached to a particular expenditure). Examples of this might be increasing specific taxes for education. The same types of governance tools can be used by the second jurisdiction to arrive at point A'.

Jurisdictions with strong dynamic capabilities also have an advantage. They should be able to take advantage of this to move the production possibility frontier further out, resulting in a social welfare tangency at a higher level of social welfare. The technological trade-off between the public and private sectors has not changed—rather the amount of each has increased because of the dynamic capacity of the jurisdiction. Note that the citizens' tastes and preferences have not changed but rather the ability of the jurisdiction to satisfy these has increased.

Bibliography

Bator, F. M. (1957, March). The simple analytics of welfare maximization. *American Economic Review, XLVII*(1), 22–59.

Index

J. Chapman, *The Local Budget as a Complex System*, Palgrave Studies in Public Debt, Spending, and Revenue, https://doi.org/10.1007/978-3-030-94903-7

The manufacturer's authorised representative in the EU is Springer Nature Customer Service Centre GmbH, Europaplatz 3, 69115 Heidelberg, Germany. If you have any concerns regarding our products, please contact ProductSafety@springernature.com

Printed and bound by CPI Group (UK) Ltd, Croydon, CR0 4YY

30/09/2026

02225475-0007